The Fight In Me

Taking the Leap and Leaving the Footprints

SHERRIAN PALMER-BARTHOL

ISBN-13: 978-1-953759-73-3

Dedication

To My Parents: Norma (Mrs.) and Claude Palmer (Mr.)

Dear Mom and Dad,

From whom I'm made alive. The core of who I am, the root and source of my strength. There is no number of words that I can ever say that you will ever be able to comprehend how much you both mean to me. I myself just cannot fathom how two people make so many dreams and hope of mine come to life: without judgement, just support. All that I am and all that I will ever be will forever be because of such great foundation that you both have built for our family. I have never lacked anything that I ever need to birth any of my dreams. You both have supported my journeys in every way you know how to. I am forever indebted to you both. The plethora of sacrifices that were made for me has never once gone unnoticed. Thank you, mom and Dad, for a beautiful life. I hope I have done justice to our name and somehow made you both proud. Happy 46th year of togetherness mom and dad and happy 25th year wedding anniversary. I love you both to the moon and back. Always and forever.

Your daughter,
Sherrian Palmer-Barthol

Special Thanks

Every now and then we all need a helping hand through this crazy journey we call life. Writing a book is not without its challenges. Especially for a first-time writer as myself. There were a lot of nights I would break down in tears from revisiting the past. To my Husband, Billy Barthol (III) Thank you for being my main support system. Sometimes it's bringing me dinner in the office, massaging my back after a long night of writing or a hug in those moments when I get frustrated. My parents and siblings, thank you all for never doubting this dream of mine but always finding ways to support me. For keeping the prayer chain going on my behalf and mentioning my name and journey every time to God. To my three best friends: Andriana, Samiesha and Tashona thank you for the motivation daily, the push to bring this dream to life and the confidence you all have shown in me. To my publisher Mr. C. Orville McLeish, thank you for your patience with me and bringing my dream to reality.

The Fight In Me

Taking the Leap and Leaving the Footprints

SHERRIAN PALMER-BARTHOL

Table of Contents

Introduction

If I had put my life in a song, you would have said I am using my voice to impress you, and all the tremor of my vocals would not be enough to move you. So, I am putting it all in words: write it down, scribble it, scratch it down whatever it may; because I swear that every single word is true. Whether I am a role model to some or not, the life I live will surely tell. Despite its title, this book does not portray any form of violence or any type of physical encounter with another. However, in some instances and situations I did feel as though that was my first resort. My strong-willed mindset has always granted me the courage to fight through all the darts life has thrown my way. The will to persevere, the determination to succeed and the drive to keep going; amidst all odds and every established generational trait and practice has always kept me on my toes. Simply put, its diving headfirst into what you believe in and putting in the work to bring it to reality. For whatever reason you may happen to hear these phrases: you will never amount to anything in life, you will fail, or you are worthless, then you may have an idea of what a shattered heart feels like. And just like that, you lose interest in socializing with others, you began to question your self-esteem. All that you have ever done becomes vain to your own eyes and you wish you had not woken up the next day. But, if every one of those days you woke up with the determination and the urge to fight through that pain and gather the courage to fight one last time and have one last cry then you'd be surprised to know how big your heart is. Even if you yourself thought they shattered it beyond repair, what really happens is that they have taught you how to be strong. You found strength in places you did not even know existed.

Chapter One

THE FOUNDATIONS

S temming from a Christian home, the act of prayer has always been one of our family's core values. As a child growing up, waking up at 4:30 AM was a requirement and not an option. No question asked, that is final. Why would a child have to wake up that early you may wonder, when school starts at 8:30 AM? The answer is to attend our daily prayer meetings in the living room. I can still hear my mom's feet dragging into my bedroom that I shared with my sister that is two years older than me and my cousin that my mom raised. That is a sound that never goes away.

"Wake up, wake up, prayer meeting time" is my mom's signature phrase. I dragged myself out of bed with my blanket still wrapped around my body as the morning wind makes its way through every crack and crevice of our poorly structured house. My mind still in slumber, I threw myself onto the couch and rolled into a ball. The frustration I felt could be seen on my face and in all my actions, but that did not stop my mom from asking me to lead the morning devotion.

Our morning sessions would last for about 30 minutes and occasionally when my mom decides to pray for our entire community by name, then that is another 15 minutes. Nothing excites me as a child than hearing the last Amen, because now I can get to go back to bed for another hour of sleep until 6AM to get ready for School. I flew up out of the couch faster than I sat, bursting with joy only to hear my mom say, "nobody nuh go back inna di bed, nuh wata nuh deh yah, unuh go dun a river".

At this point my heart dropped, I could not decide how to feel in the moment. I wanted to cry so bad, but I just did not want to hear the "I might give you something to cry for" speech. Thus, I picked up my 12-quart water jug, a black plastic bag with my bath soap, wash cloth, toothpaste and toothbrush, underwear and started our five minutes' walk to the river. Day had just started to break and the morning wind blowing from the west, slaps itself up against my face, making an already blurry vision blurrier. Having to take a shower in a 35-degree temperature and freezing chilly water was not fun, but that was our morning routine for most of our lives.

I was always a smart mouth and as such I started basic school at an incredibly early age. I was two years old when I stepped out in my red and white plaid, pleated uniform to attend the Mount Hindmost basic school. I really do not have a lot of memories about my early years but what I can tell you is that I was the boss. I tried to rule everyone big or small, I never took orders from kids my age and I was not afraid to discipline any one of them when they slack up. I got baptized in June 2000 at two years old. I was born in the church, if you may say as my mom gave her life to Christ when I was two years old. Being baptized at that early age did not stop me from being rude to whoever I chose or act any different as a kid, because of course I did not understand what it is to be baptized. However, in Sunday school my hand was always up to recite a bible verse or to sing a song. I will have to be the person with the microphone or else I will not take part. I have always been a God-fearing child growing up and willing to do anything in the church.

14

The church was one of the two places on my mom's "to go" list away from school. Amidst the fact that I got baptized from an incredibly early age and didn't understand the dynamics of being a Christian, I am extremely glad my mom let me because it did prepare me for my later years as a young adult growing up. My earlier years went by extremely fast as there was not anything for me to consider about more than just live. I graduated top of my class from elementary with certificates for most outstanding, most helpful, and most discipline. I knew from the start that I could be great but what I did not know was that I would have to fight as hard as I did. I did not know that I was going to be challenged, spiritually, emotionally, financially and socially. Put in the fire to be tested and come out with a lot of bruises.

I have lived a very humble life, below the poverty line some may say where food, shelter and clothing as a necessity for humans to survive was lacking in more than one instance for us. But God has always been there for us, he always showed up on time. To say we were hungry would be a lie, but there were times as a kid I did not have the luxury of choosing what to eat. I had to bless and eat what my parents provided for me, even if it is the same thing the seven days of the week.

My dad has had some bad hits by drought where our livelihood was threatened. There was a time when all we had was some incredibly old cassava that my dad has not harvested in years that we had to dig up and use to make bammy for breakfast, lunch and dinner. This meal was prepared by gratering this plant root that is packed with carbohydrates, then taking a piece of cloth to ring as much juice out of it as possible. My dad would now take the dry shredded root and flattened it out into a Dutch pot to bake for a couple minutes on both sides and then sprinkle it with a little salt. As the baby in the family at the time, my parents would make sure I got the first one as my other siblings sat around the fire and waited for theirs.

15

We could not afford to buy a gas stove, so our primary method of cooking was wood fire outside on a homemade fire bed that my dad built with bamboo, zinc and three stones. Occasionally we would have charcoal as well that my dad burned in a kiln. Think of the structure of the fireplace as a little table, but with a tiny little shed to keep off any excess rain. If the idea of having to cook outside with wood is not already overwhelming, then think about grabbing a machete and a piece of rope to go gather some wood to pack under that table.

As corny as it sounds, we do specialize in the type of wood that we use. Orange wood and pimento wood are two of our specialties. These kinds of wood last an extraordinarily long time. Unlike mango wood which gives off a lot of smoke and requires a lot of human strength to be blowing all the time just to get some flames. I used to get terrible migraines from constantly blowing the fire and getting smoked directly into my eyes for hours. We would head out to an orange field and try to gather as much wood as we can carry to stack up under our little shed. With my dad having a chainsaw, sometimes my brothers would just drop an entire dry pimento tree and share the weight on their shoulders to bring it home and that would last us for a little while.

Livestock has been in my family for all my life. But in trying times things can really get rough for everyone. The drought does not just affect our crops, but it affects the food for our animals, the grass and the river, their main water source. When the grass field began to wither it put our livestock at such a substantial risk, as they were not able to graze. I remember we lost over 30 chickens due to dehydration and a massive heat wave. That was so heart rending because that is how we survive. Fishing supplies protein in our family. Whether it is catching fish, shrimp, eel or whatever edible freshwater protein that we can source from the river. But when drought hits, even that is threatened as the rivers dry out in most areas and water shortage is now a detrimental concern. The river is our main source of water. To drink, for domestic purposes, animal rearing and plants.

Being the youngest child at the time, I was everyone is favorite. My dad and I have always been close, we have formed an unbreakable bond which most times makes my elder siblings jealous I would think. I have known my dad to be a farmer and a worker on the sugar plantation for as long as I can remember. Whatever that could be grown in our climate my dad has it on his farm. Farming is vital for our family as that is our biggest source of income alongside animal rearing. Some examples include chicken, goat, pigs and birds, and a donkey for our means of transporting water or our crops from the bush.

My dad working on the sugar plantation has been one of the toughest jobs I would say. If it rains or shines the work must go on. My mom would normally prepare his lunch and have us take it to him when school is out. I look at his face and all I see is pain. His skin glitters as gold as the burning sun causes the sweat to drip off his body. My dad worked on the sugar plantation for over 40 years until a couple of years ago when us kids decided that it's time for him to quit, as he no longer had a baby to take care of as my younger sister was just out of high school. He knew within himself that he wanted to stop working on the sugar farm, but he could not stop when he still had a kid to put through school. Family has always been a priority to all of us. No words that I will ever write will be able to do my parents justice for all that they have done for me and all of us as kids.

Whenever my dad is not on the plantation, he is at his farm preparing the land for planting, grooming or harvesting. This has always been a family effort. There is always one weekend appointed where we would go to the bush as a family knowing we are going to get the assigned tasks done. My mom would load up the donkey with a couple pots, water, food to cook and plates. While the men clean the land, the women would share

17

the task of cooking and searching through the bush for anything that could be harvested at the time. Whenever it is planting time the men in the family dig the holes and we drop the seeds. When it is time for harvesting, especially in the mango season that starts June and ends early September, it has always been a bittersweet time for us as kids, especially me.

For everything there is a routine. They said early birds catch the most worm and my mom proves that to me all the time. We would wake up 5 am every morning to start our thirty minutes hike up some very strenuous hills to reap ripe mangoes. We have no specific containers for this task, it is just about anything we find around the house; bath pans, water buckets, feed bags it does not matter. What matters was that we are coming home with mangoes ready for my mom to take to the market to sell. I did not know I could climb until I was twelve years old, and my mom sent me up into a mango tree to fill up a bucket with mangoes.

At the time I was not thinking about falling. All I knew was that I was going to do whatever it takes so food was on our table. If you are thinking about my five feet two inches height, no worries because my mom has just the thing for me. My dad built these geniuses catch bags for us. It is just a feed bag attached to a stick with a wire running through the mouth of the bag to keep it open. For the limbs that look too dangerous for us we would use that bag to shake the limbs and then the mangoes would fall inside the bag. The good in what looks like such a hard-strenuous task is that you can just sit in a mango tree and eat as many mangoes as you wish, after you finish filling up the containers. On the downside of that, trying to load up a thirty to fifty-pound weight container filled with ripe mangoes, onto your head after consuming so many mangoes are not an easy task. The relief I feel after stepping through our gate and unloading that container is priceless. That is a sigh of accomplishment.

Sadly, for me that is not final. I would now help in picking out the best of the batch in the afternoon after school and after we have dinner and repacked in a well cushioned container padded with grass to keep them from bruises. We would sit in our outside kitchen for hours in the dark with a flashlight or a kerosine lamp. As seconds turned into minutes and minutes into hours we would have now been out there in the dark until 10 pm. My mom would head out for the market around 5:30 Am. If she is just going to deliver a bunch of mangoes for an order, she receives then that would just take an hour or two to get back, but if she must sell everyone by herself then that could take quite a few hours. It is summer, so schools are out. Long days without my mom in the yard can wear down on me sometimes.

The sound of any vehicles coming down the driveway makes my heartbeat in hopes that it is my mom. If it is not, I remember I would start crying and sit on an old tire out by the gate that my sister planted a flower plant in. I would plant my face in my lap while my mind is fixed on my mom, hoping she is safe and hope she had a good sale day because that would mean we would be eating good the next day for dinner and one of us getting a new flip flop, a shirt or some underwear.

The sound of empty containers knocking up against the trunk of a car woke me up from my sobbing, and there my mom was, with the biggest smile on her face to see me waiting at the gate for her. I would rush to go grab one of the containers because they were not coming back home empty on a good sales day. They are packed with groceries to last us another two weeks. This process of harvesting and selling would continue throughout the year, with whatever there is to bring to the market. It is a hectic task but non the less, an extremely rewarding one.

The above-mentioned scenarios are some of, but not limited to the things that sets our family's foundation. The act of doing what it takes to better not ourselves but all members in our household. The values instilled in me from an incredibly early age, still influence my current everyday life. It is seen in the way I treat every individual, my common courtesy and even my actions as a wife. The bond between my siblings and I have always been a close one, even though disagreements, arguments or me just acting like a smart mouth for the most part. I was always raised to sincerely apologize to my elder siblings and they in return were taught to treat me with respect amidst the fact that I was the baby.

My family is in no place to judge another family because we have had our fair shares of trials and tribulation. What I will say sets us apart from every other family I know is the parenting skills of my parents. They were hated by many because they were too strict, especially my mom. Growing up, Church and School were the only places I didn't need to ask their permission to go, but everywhere else would need their approval, thus I don't bother to ask because the answer is no. It does not matter were. I was not allowed to have sleepovers or spend time at a friend's house. Ridiculous right? The same thing I thought then.

But growing up and seeing the woman I have become I would not be anywhere close, if all these privileges were granted to me. And for that I want to say thank you mom. Thank you for seeing me through your own eyes. You saw what I needed, what was going to hurt me and what was best for me, and you protected me from them and led me to what was best. Secondly, the moment my mom gave her life to Christ she brought all her kids with her. She would normally say, "God give me unuh, and mi a gi unuh back to him". And as such I would say the church protected us for a long time and still is. I could have gotten pregnant at the age of thirteen just like any other female because I was not better off than any of them that fell into that trap. The church kept me focused on the world but not of the world.

Families can be each other's biggest demons, but with a good foundation, it will be able to withstand the rain and the storms. Make your foundation counts, take the time to structure it properly. Ask God for guidance if you don't know how to, because when it's all said and done and the winds of life shattered all the fancy outside structure, all you will have been the foundation to just build on again. Gather the courage to build. People are going to go against your style of building but build. They are going to criticize you for the materials you are using but build. Only you know what is best for your family and what works for mine may not work for you. It can be a scary task but trust your gut and open your ears and heart for whatever direction God has for you. Trust the process, trust in God, build with faith.

21

Chapter Two

BECOMING BETTER

Good parenting is not all about clothing your child in the latest brands or supplying them with all the trending devices and gadgets. Especially for first time moms, you want to give your kids the world if it will make them happy. However, that alone will never be enough to suffice a child. Preparing them for a bitter world that is just waiting to devour them and seeing them master each obstacle with the tools and knowledge you have provided them with is far more satisfying. It is like planting an Apple tree. You spend days molding and nurturing it just in time for it to put forth fruits. You watch the drought come and burn all the leaves, see the floods come and toss it to and from but the root stays firm.

Doesn't it make you want to plant more of its kind because you have seen how well it withstands hard and treacherous conditions? Yes, it does. The same applies to raising a child. You have given them all you can as a mother and a father, you nurture, love and care for them with everything within you. You have watched them grow up and come of a certain age where your parenting skills are going to be tested by the fire. But you watch them use the resources you have given them and come out stronger than ever, that is amongst one of the proudest moments as a mom.

Growing up I did not have the luxury of wearing the latest brand clothing, better yet I did not have much clothing. Hand-Me-Down was my go-to. In lame man's term these are clothing that my elder sister wore and passed down to the next younger sister until I was able to fit in them. Thankfully, I wore uniforms to school, so I did not have to worry about wearing the only two suits I have 365 days. My mom would buy the material with the sales money from the market and my bigger sister Kay would sew my uniforms. Currently, I have the luxury of buying the style, color and shape of the type of underwear I want in bundles.

As a young girl and teenager even, those sometimes come in Hand-Me-Down, sadly but it was what it was. Or the other choice was that I only have three that is originally mine. The worst part about this underwear is the fact that everyone is going to know what it is. The fact is because all of us sisters are varied sizes by the time it reaches me. I had to tie the sides for it to fit, leaving these big bumps showing through my clothes. After every shower I would wash that one for the next day. There is one thing to note though, even though I did not have a lot of clothing my mom made sure I was exceptionally clean. She ensures that good hygiene is practiced and enforced.

I used to complain because I think I should have more. More clothing, more room space instead of sharing with my sister Roxann and my cousin Jody-kaye. It feels all wrong and unfair until my mom would just sit with me and have casual conversations. Sharing with me what life was for her and my dad and as a kid growing up. After listening to her first sentence, I at once started getting emotional and apologized for how I acted sometimes. I have never had to cut grass to make my bed, I never use a flour bag for clothing or grater dried coconut to make coconut oil for cooking. I will admit, my current lifestyle was not great by any means, but it was by far better than that of my parents.

I humbly sat there and sobbed as I listened to more of my mom's past lifestyle. I could hear the pain in her voice as she said these words to me. "I have ten kids, one dead left nine. Mi start having pickney exceedingly early at 19 years old cause I never knew better. Mi never get fi go a nuh high school, mi affi tie pan a mi side and throw fertilizer and run wid fruit basket pon mi head. Unuh come better time dan mi, so you better take God and tek you book. Mi wants all a unuh fi better than mi and unuh daddy, none a unuh nuh fi come wuk a sharp property, dats why mi spend mi last dime fi mek sure seh unuh get the schooling weh mi nuh get, so do mi a beg you nuh waste it". After this speech I could not continue sobbing so I just burst out in tears. The anger I felt towards myself is indescribable but at the same time I never felt more loved and cared for after hearing those words, which helped me to realize that, yes, they would love for me to have tons of clothes and everything to my comfort, but they could have only done that and so much.

At 6 years old I started attending the John Austin All Age school starting at grade one. It consisted of nine grades at the time of my attendance. Transportation to school was not a concern as we lived less than quarter of a mile away from the school. It has always been a fun trip to and from school as we would travel in groups consisting of cousins and neighbors. School begins at 8:30 AM. One of my parents' biggest concerns was that we have breakfast before school. Even if it were an overnight cold dumpling that my dad had on his plate, I would eat it and head out to school. I have always loved school but hearing my parents talk about their past motivates me to study harder than the average student because I refuse to relive their past experiences. I was not a fussy child growing up, for reasons that most of the time I did not have a choice in what I wear or what I eat, so if there was someone that wanted to share something to me there was a low possibility of me refusing it.

Over time the school system changes, and they start providing free breakfast to the students. It was a bittersweet moment for me, but it makes my parents happy knowing for sure that I would not be hungry at school. Standing in the line with my big red bowl ready to collect my cornmeal porridge, it felt as though all eyes were fixed on me and they were. As I walked to my classroom in shame, I could hear the chatter and gossip and some even publicly mocked and humiliated me because I was the poor girl whose parents could not provide breakfast. A Lot of tears fell into those bowls of porridge as I continued to bear the shame and keep collecting free breakfast.

For the average kid, their lunch would be a side of fruits with a sandwich, a juice and chips. For me it was a couple of fry fritters wrapped up in a piece of the paper flour bag with some sugar and water or on good days it would be an Austin biscuit and pineapple syrup. If you think walking away with my porridge and getting stares and undertone gossip was humiliating it is nothing compared to what happened next. I could not eat my lunch in peace inside the classroom. I would have to hide behind the neighboring church, inside a bell house. Kids would laugh at what I was eating and mocked me for the entirety of the day. Some even went as far as picking up my lunch and started passing it around to their friends. Unbelievably, I was not a 'walk over' in school. I talk back and I have a whole lot of attitudes, but the only thing that kept me from lashing out at these kids were my parents and knowing what they stand for.

The above-mentioned scenario was getting out of control and was starting to affect me emotionally, so as a mother my mom tried to find a new way to make sure I was comfortable. She would prepare the same lunch, but this time around have me come home when it was lunch time, eat and go back to school. That did work on the one end that kids stopped messing with me, but on the other end it was draining physically even though it was not too far away. Through all of this, my grades never drop. I worked harder and twice as much as everyone else. I had a goal insight, and I was not going to let anything, or anyone let me lose sight of it. All that I had faced and have endured were just to test my patience and I always ended up the winner.

Around grade five my mom discovered an even better way to provide lunch for me that would not have me laughed at, neither was it physically and mentally exhausting. At this point in our life things got a little better, life overall was better. My mom would buy Styrofoam lunch boxes and make rice and peas and stew chicken, steam fish among many other kinds of meat for my lunch. She would fix it up nicely, the same way and better than the cook shops were selling. On days when she did not wake up early enough to make me lunch, she would make it while I was at school and at lunch time, she would meet me halfway with my freshly homemade lunch. Not all heroes wear cape because my mom and my dad are the greatest heroes I know.

Now the tables were turned. I have classmates flocking my lunch wanting to taste and request that my mother made some extras for them the next day. I have classmates giving me their lunch money in exchange for my food and because I have always been a smart girl, I took their money. I would then bring it home to my parents to contribute more food for my lunch the next day. At this point in time, I had already garnered a lot of hate and resentment towards my classmates, so I might have been angry, but I was not stupid. I keep collecting their money for the food I would take to school, but my mom would take the money and insist I stop collecting from the kids because she provided for them freely.

My mom would always reference psalms 118:22, "The stone that the builder refused has been the head stone of the corner". At 11 years old I did not understand much of what it truly meant, but I would always nod my head in agreement with my mom whenever she said it. For all I knew then it meant people that used to trash talk and even trash my lunch are now even going to limits as wanting to purchase it from me. God has been good! He works in mysterious ways, ways in which we cannot fathom. It was from that money I received I started operating a small business by buying wafers and selling them to the entire school, even to teachers. Whatever profit I would receive I would save. I did this for two years and I never regret doing it. It paid for trips, projects and school resources my parents could not afford.

Can you relate to being in similar situations and you watch God pull you through? Sometimes all I can do in the moment is saying, "but God you nuh easy enuh". I am always astonished at the ways God works. What seems like it was a dire situation for me, the last thread, my breaking point was all a part of God's main plan. I for one found myself guilty of asking the "Why me?" question. When things stop going my way and with my plan it always feels as though the world is against me. But for God's will to be done he has to take us out of our comfort zone. When we are most vulnerable to break, to throw in the towels and call it quits, he always shows up for us and gives us a crown of beauty for Ashes. You are his masterpiece and do not let anyone tell you otherwise.

My first term in grade six I participated in my first spelling bee competition. I was probably short of a spelling bee book and a little practice but not confidence and motivation. My mother was my biggest fan. I was put up against much older students in the competition, but I was never scared or intimidated. I did not bring home the first place, neither the second-place trophy but I did come in third. At the time it did not matter if I had lost. I felt like a winner because I was brave enough to challenge persons with more experiences than myself. I brought home the certificate of award to my mom and that smile I received was all the validation I needed. This was not my first award certificate since I started this school but this one meant more to her because she knew I lacked the resources necessary for the task and she could not give it to me. However, she noticed my urge and determination so we would practice from an old beat-up oxford dictionary that was given to my elder sister. Thus, me coming in at third place was an immensely proud moment for us.

Transitioning into grade six can be a lot of pressure. At this grade, I was put to the test in 5 subject areas: mathematics, English language, Science, Social Studies and Communication Skills. I see this phase as the place where your dreams start manifesting into reality. Primary schools across Jamaica host this national exam annually, Grade Six Achievement Test (GSAT). Based on your scores you are then placed into a High School that is compatible with your marks. This was important for me as I chose the top five schools in my Parish, Clarendon. Preparing for my exams was stressful because I did not really know what to expect, I had to trust my teacher in hopes that what we revised was what I was going to see on the paper. My teacher would host these marathons and extra classes and I would miss so many because my parents could not afford it. I would hide outside the windows and take notes as the class was going on. One day I got rotted out by classmates and my teacher, Ms. Robathom invited me inside, such a blessing in disguise. She realizes how eager I was to learn but I just could not afford it. Since that day I have attended every marathon, every extra class, no charge!

Finally, the big day arrived. My mom woke early that morning to make me my favorite breakfast. She knew how anxious I was, so she stared at me and said, "you ago alright man, left it to God" and just like that all anxiety went away. I remember sitting in the exam room just praying for about five minutes. I was raised to pray about everything. It was now the last exam, and everybody started chattering on how well they did and which high school they think they are going to. I

29

grabbed my little zip locker bag containing my eraser and pencils and headed straight home. No conversation, nothing. Am I not an optimistic individual and ambitious as everyone else? I sure am. But I was taught to never exalt myself.

And thus, I waited patiently for the results. Back in 2007, the results were given publicly in our morning devotions which the entire school attended. Your name would be called followed by the high school you are going to attend. High schools in Jamaica are categorized based on scores. So, to go to one of the best high schools you would then have to make sure your scores matched their requirements. I leaned against the wall waiting for the principal to get to the letter "P" since the results are in alphabetical order. One of my best friends, Tashona Ellis, had already heard of her pass and was super excited because that was our first choice and we wanted to attend the same High School. It was a nerve-racking experience as I held on to my other best friend, Samiesha Stobbs who was also a nerve wreck.

The principal finally made it to "P" and my name was first on the list. My heart raced as she called my name but more so waiting to hear which High School. "Sherrian Palmer, Edwin Allen High School" the principal lamented. I jumped and screamed, hugging my best friends as Tash and I both got to go to the same high school. Before we were even finished screaming, we heard "Samiesha Stobbs, Edwin Allen High School". At that moment we all started crying. I was very emotional because I got to continue my journey in school with my best friends, but that was not all.

Growing up my parents always shared with me how much they did not make it to High School because their parents thought it was best for them to work in the fields, and as such they would miss a lot of school days and just drop out. They shared how ignorant the idea was and how much they would never do it to their children. My mom used to tell me, "I am not a good reader because I did not get much schooling, I did not make it past primary school. So please I am begging you, take all the learning you can". Those words never just came through one ear and out the other, they stayed with me up until this day. After hearing of my passing, it was in that moment I knew I had made my parents proud once more. All the sacrifices they have made are now paid off; my mother's prayer did not go in vain. I have become better. Better than my parent's past, better than the expectations people held me to, better than anything I could imagine. And ever since then, all I have ever been BETTER!!

High School was not a bed of roses. Challenges were ever present from the start to the finish. As proud as my parents were for me and excited that I got to start a different and better chapter of my life, it is without a doubt that they were scared as well. Scared for not being able to provide me with the necessary tools to complete my studies as financial challenges can be very tough sometimes.

The Program of Advancement Through Health and Education (PATH) has been of immense help throughout my high school learning. With this program I was able to go to school and not worry about lunch. At the time, the transportation fare by the bus was one hundred and forty dollars round trip (around 14US$ at the time) and travelled for 18 miles to and from. Most mornings I left home with just one hundred and fifty dollars to my name. It was hard, but not as hard as not getting the opportunity to further my education, compared to my parents.

In every aspect of high School, challenges present themselves. My eldest sister, Kay, had to make my uniform twice my size. That way I can have it for a couple more years. I did not have the luxury of choosing which brand bags or shoes I want to wear to school. I must thank my parents and be grateful. To this very day I still do not know how I made it through High School. It is only God! From burnt out uniforms, to my shoes bottom falling off in front a bunch of students as if that was not humiliating enough. They laughed and mocked me, but it did not last long. Being poor but intelligent is such a game changer.

People are always going to talk about you, whether it is good or bad. And that is a concept I had to learn fast. Have you ever felt as though everything you have ever done is always a problem to someone or a group of people? I have been there on several occasions. I used to question my actions, took a couple steps back and reevaluated my decisions, to figure out where I misstep or overstepped. Only come to find out that people are intimidated by your intelligence and your success. They only want to see one instance of a possibility of you becoming better than what they hope, what they thought or what they think you should be, you then become an instant problem. But take it from me, through it all NEVER STOP BECOMING BETTER.

Chapter Three

FRIENDSHIP JOURNEY

T eenage years are either the best or the worst time of your life. It is exceedingly rare when you weigh the good and the bad and they are equally balanced. From firsthand experiences I have had an awesome teenage life with a few downfalls, which many would classified as the typical teenager phase, but I cannot help but think they were just stupid decisions and dumb mistakes. Are we still talking about the girl who attended only school and church related events, having an awesome teenager experience? No smoking? No drinking? No partying etc.? Yes, we are still talking about her. The examples mentioned described the typical fun events for a teenager but somehow none of that was not fun to me, better yet I was not allowed to affiliate with persons of such groups. What made my teenage years so good was the friends I had and still have.

For most if not all my younger years, I have been very naive and oblivious of who is a friend. At the time, I thought that because I am genuinely nice to a person and they smiled back at me, they are now my friend. I just could not understand why they were not always my friend. I have had cases where a family member would tell me to be careful of a certain "friend" and I would question the reason behind telling me, because to me I was very polite and nice to that person, I have done no harm, so why should I take precautions? I would have gone on to learn that people are not always what they seem to be.

I can recall an instance of a bad friendship that my parents and I constantly had arguments for a whole week because of heresies. For an entire week, my routine was waking up, going to school then coming home to heresies. This has been one of the roughest weeks in my entire life. This person was not only a "friend" but was also family. I was around twelve years old at the time and I can remember laying in my room, eyes fixed on the ceiling, my sinuses draining all over my face and through the tears and pain I muttered, "I will never ever call someone my friend again". I woke up the next morning with a whole new mindset and a distinct perspective on life, but what I did not know was that I was going to meet two people who were going to help me get over my hurt and show me that loyal friends do exist.

It was the morning of September fourth, 2006. It was my last first day of primary school. New uniforms, new shoes, nice hairstyle was enough to be stoked about at twelve years old. What I did not remember, was that I was going to meet a whole new class of students since I repeated grade six, since I was too young to do the GSAT the previous year. Therefore, all the familiar faces are gone on to high school. I once said I have no idea what it is to be the new student, but thinking about it now, even though they are moving into grade six which I was already, I was the only stranger. So, I was technically the new student.

Devotion had just been dismissed and students dispersed to their respective classes. I walked into a classroom filled with strangers. I watched everyone find their cliques and their little groups while I stood close to the chalkboard waiting for everyone to be seated for me to get a view of a vacant seat. It was extremely hard to find a vacant seat because there was not any single seating in place. There were benches and desks that seats four people. So, I walked off trying to bury my pride to ask if I could sit with a certain group when I heard, "New girl you want to sit with us?" said Samiesha Stobbs (kk). My anxiety level increased very quickly. I walked over and sat beside her making five people seated at that desk. I looked around and there were a couple benches that I could sit more comfortably on. I wanted to move but I did not want to be rude and disrespectful since she was the only person who offered me a seat.

My first instinct was, wow this girl is so nice I really want to be her friend. My immediate reflex was like, "no way, remember people aren't always what they seem, no friends". I immediately shut down. I became quiet and started overthinking. Is this girl trying to get close to me to do me ill? What is her motive? Why did not she just leave me alone? I became overprotective of who I let close to me due to one unpleasant experience. For me one was too many and I never wanted to experience anything like it ever again.

Well, I made it through the first day of school smooth. Better than I expected. We said goodbye and went our separate ways. There was something remarkably familiar with one of the new girls, Tashona Ellis. (Tash). We were both walking in the same direction home. I tried to brainstorm all the possible places she might live but could not put my hand to it. I walked about 50 feet behind her in hopes of seeing where she lives, but nothing. I came to my lane, and she was still going. I walked up to the nearby shop and watched her and finally she opened a gate. I was shocked! How did I not know she lived beside my god father and I'm always there? But thinking about it that house was recently built, and that family recently moved into it from a different area of the community.

The next day I made it to school early to get a more comfortable seat. I sat there waiting for class to begin only to see Tash walking in my direction. I said to myself, "oh no, not again" Hey, come sit with us again, we have a seat for you" she said. I replied, "are you sure?" she nods her head saying yes. So, I picked up my bag and went to sit with them. It was very noticeable though that one of the girls was no longer there. Did they just ditch one of their friends for me? Will they ditch me next for someone else? I could not help but ask about her, then I learned she was just sitting with them for the day as she has her own group of friends who was not present on the first day of school. Ever since then I have sat on that same bench for an entire year with the same faces.

School ended once more, but the only difference is we did not just split up and went our way. we learned of each other's place of abode. Came to find out we were all loners. KK lived closest to school on a hill in a neighboring community while Tash and I lived about one hundred feet apart in a different community, all walking distance to School. This specific evening, we all held hands walking out the school gate. Kk soon came upon her detour. She looked at me and said, "you want to follow me go halfway" I quickly agreed. Tash was not so fond of it as it was just extra walking. However, she walked with us. On top of the hill was a little track that would take Tash and I back onto our road instead of going all the way around back. We came half of the way and were getting ready to say goodbye. All I felt was a tighter grip onto my hand as she said, "Just a little closer". And before we knew it, we followed her all the way home. Lol. we both had a laugh and Tash said, "never again".

This routine has now become our usual minus the fact that it was only me falling for KK's trap as Tash was incredibly determined she was not coming ever again. After the third time you would have thought that I had learned my lesson and not fall for it right? My dumb ass still followed her. One day Tash came up with a brilliant idea. We held hands as usual but this time we put KK in the middle and forced her to walk with us halfway and then took the track back to her house and it did work. Ever Since then we have been accompanying each other half the way home. At this point our friendship was remarkably

36

close and I started opening back little by little while keeping some more sensitive walls up.

Growing up in the Mount Hindmost District community, there was not anything much to do as a teenager. The river was one thing that Tash and I have in common. We both love to swim and love being at the river. At twelve years old I was already washing my own clothes at the river. Tash was not so much as she was the baby of her family, and her mommy wants to do it. When she learnt that I go to the river every Saturday morning at six in the morning, she started coming with me to do her own laundry as well. Another routine was formed and maintained for as long as I can remember.

As time goes by, I keep getting closer and closer with these girls. Tash and I started attending church together, hanging out at each other's houses and all. On weekends I would lie about going to the library for schoolwork and ended up at KK's house. I would spend a couple of hours and leave in time to be in line with the library's closing time. I was happy that I got the chance to hang out with her, but my heart raced as I was walking from her house in hopes that no one saw me or knew me or my parents. Because then, I would receive a fine whopping for lying to my parents and future library privileges would be taken away from me. It went well for the time being until my mom met KK and learnt about our growing friendship. My parents had already met Tash and knew that she was coming from a loving home. This was like a jackpot for me that my parents approved and loved my potential friends. Yes, I was still not letting my guard down fully.

It was like a miracle. It happens so fast. How did I go from thinking that they could be potential friends to calling them my best friends? Yes, you heard me, my best friends. Almost a year has gone by since meeting them. It was time to start high school and all three of us were going to the same high school. We were overwhelmed with joy to know we were not going to be separated after forming such a great friendship. What was going to happen next was going to shock us all.

It is bad enough when your best friend is going to a whole different high school. How bad can a different class be? Well, bad. Our high school required us to take some tests prior to the semester. The grades earned would then place us in different classes. Guess who did not get placed with the other two. You guessed wrong, not me. It was KK. she was placed in the A stream while Tash and I was in the B stream. I could not help but feel like fate was pulling away KK from me.

Why is it that I get to live so close to only Tash, why not both? Why do not I have more leisure time with her? Why do they place her in a different class away from us? Is she going to find new friends and forget us? Is she ever going to talk to us again? Will she come see us sometime? Who is she going to eat lunch with? I know! I know! It is petty, it is childish. But I could not help but feel as though I was about to lose one of my best friends. A friend that took me over one year to build a good foundation and give friendship a second shot.

It was our first day at high school. It is usually a super exciting day for the most part. For us it was not so exciting. We have moments when we totally forgot about the situation and we would have a laugh, but it wouldn't last exceedingly long. We went to our classes and could not help but think about what each other was doing. Sounds like a committed relationship, right? Well, that is how much we devoted ourselves in maintaining our friendship.

Tash and I could not wait for our first break, because we wanted to go look for KK. we did not know she was thinking the same thing as well. "Ding-ding-ding" the bell echoed. We stormed out of our seat as fast as we could. We made it to our classroom doors and all we saw was this tiny little girl with the longest legs making her way to our direction. We met in the middle and hugged each other. We went back to Tash and me classroom and gossiped about which teachers we liked and did not like, new people we met and possible crushes. Ever Since then we go back and forth to each other's classes to have lunch. By now you would have known that once a pattern is established between us, it is maintained. So, we go on to have evening routines, what bus we take, what time we meet in the square to go to school, what we buy for lunch, who is holding who in their lap the next morning, we have routines for everything. There was this one old lady "Aunty" who owned a little shop in our town. Once we got off the bus in the afternoon that is our first stop. Kk would do the honor of buying a five-dollar bag juice and cheese trix for all three of us. And of course, we became "Aunties' favorite customer because we make it an everyday thing.

This may not be much to some, but to us it was everything. It was the thought that was put into it. It is the closeness, the unity and love it brings to our friendship. There were so many things we must fight through as a unit. People could not understand why we have almost a perfect friendship, so they start passing judgements and gossiping. I had a lady once ask if I had any future goals of ever becoming a joint unit with another female. Wow!! What a fancy way to assume that I am Bi-Sexual or a lesbian. This was a hard pillow to swallow for all of us, but we got through together.

There were a lot of stereotypes which we faced. Fourteen years old and no boyfriend? Wow! I wonder why? They must be lesbians. It was bizarre. At fourteen years old I was still a baby in my parents' eyes and secondly, having a boyfriend meant that I would have to pack my stuff and leave my parents' house, never talk to them again, my siblings would be disappointed in me, and I wouldn't be welcomed at my parents' house anymore. For me family was everything. If you would recall earlier, I mentioned that a good family foundation is everything. It was those promises and guidelines that were mentioned that pops up in my head every time the teenager within me then wants to act a fool.

Our friendship mostly consists of spending time together at school. Except for the weekends when Tash and I would hang out at the river. KK is always a homebody plus, just like my mom does not let me hang out, KK's mom was and still is an extremely strict, respectable woman. I will forever love you, Ms. Christine. Tash's mom was a little more lenient, we went back and forth to each other's house and Tash's mom, Ms. Yvette always treats me like a blood daughter.

High school went by so fast. It was now September of 2009, and we are moving to 9th grade. We were super excited as Tash, and I got promoted to the A stream. So, this means we were all going to be in most classes together. The first week of school went by smoothly as we preplanned where we were going to sit in each class and which teachers we want to be selected for our classes. That weekend we all hung out at the library doing schoolwork and having the typical conversations. What we did not know was that the news we were going to receive the following week was going to put our friendship to the test.

We came to our usual shop to buy 5-dollar bag juice. I offered to buy snacks that specific afternoon since KK is always buying. She yelled, "no, let me treat you guys since it will be my last evening". "Your last evening?" I asked. She said, "yes, I have to tell you guys something" my heart drops. My first instinct was "oh no, here she comes. Going to ditch me or both of us" she then went on to tell us that she and her family will be migrating to the United States over the weekend. Our eyes lit up as we stared at each other for a good minute.

What exactly do I do in these moments? Should I just start crying? Can I just scream in joy for my best friend? I mean, we are talking about the USA here. Every kid in Jamaica then, wants to at least visit America moreover to live there. I still can remember we all hugged and got super excited. That afternoon we all walked to KK's house and said our last goodbye.

Our days were no longer the same. It felt as though a part of us was missing. Pun intended. At first, we continue to do everything that would remind us of her, like going to her classroom, buying snacks in the afternoon etc. Nonetheless, she was missed and there was nothing we could do about it other than cherish within our hearts all the good times we had.

Is our friendship strong enough to continue? That is an incredibly good question to ask when neither of us had a cell phone or used social media at the time. I could not help but ask myself these questions. "Have I positively impacted her life? And how easy am I to forget?" I wanted to ask my mom for a phone so bad even though I knew she would not say yes. But then again, how am I going to call KK when neither of us would have the other's number.

A year went by, and we now have our new normal. One thing never changed though; we did not replace her. Tash and I continue to be friends and do our same old same old stuff in hopes of seeing her again. Like any other Saturday morning Tash and I went to the river to wash our clothes. We came back around midday; the sun was uncomfortably hot.

Like a true country girl, I had a bunch of clothing pins pinned to my shirt, that I was going to use to hang my clothes on to the line. Did I mention that I was also barefooted? Oh yes, I was. My hair was all tangled and nappy. But who cares right? I'm home, not impressing anyone, same people I have lived with for sixteen years of my life. I did not have the slightest clue that what is going to happen next would be a game changer.

Have you ever heard of "River hunger?" it is the kind of hunger that you felt only at the river after long hours of sitting on a rock washing your clothes in a bath pan. Thus, I was just wondering round-about the house for any food or fruits that I could get to consume right away. "Sherrrrr, sherrrrr" one of my sisters called. I was so relieved I rushed to her thinking I was about to eat something. She said, "look out a gate, one of your friends a come to you". I was like, "one a mi friend, Tash and I just came from the river together".

I walked out of the room unto the veranda and popped my head at the gate. Wait a minute now! Am I dreaming? I could not believe my eyes. Walking in my direction was this slim, light skinned young lady wearing a smile so big. I stopped walking and ran straight into her arms. I felt so much emotion that day all together than I have ever felt in my entire life.

I was so stoked to see her, I was speechless, I wanted to cry. I had so many questions. When did you get here? When do you have to go back? Are you here for good? How is life in the US? Do you have a boyfriend now? I just could not stop asking the questions in my head to myself. I started getting teary and kept hugging her in between every other sentence.

Sadly, she was not going to be in the country for long. She told me the reason for her visit and that she stopped to see Tash before coming to see me. It sure did make me happy to hear her say that. She bought Tash and I matching stripe shirts. I had the green and white and Tash had the peach and white. We both wore them to spend the weekend with KK and her family and found out she had the black and white for herself.

I have accepted the fact that she will have to go back to the US, but I was not going to just let her leave like that. With no established method of communication, no nothing. Upon leaving her house we exchanged numbers. I still did not have a phone, so I gave her my mom's phone number. Goodbyes are hard but knowing that we will be able to communicate now, eases the pain a little.

I am not sure if you knew but calling the US from Jamaica and vice versa can be expensive. But what if you just want to use text messages? You are more than welcome to, but for every text message you send it will charge you six dollars off your credit. It was overwhelming, as a result we did not talk as much as we thought we would.

What changed it all for us was Facebook. We joined Facebook in 2010. The library was now my happy place as I did not have the internet at home. We took all our conversations to Facebook messenger. It was a good feeling. From time-to-time KK and her family would visit Jamaica and I would have then got phone privileges. She wanted to be in Jamaica for our high school graduation but unfortunately could not make it.

For every aspect of my life, I have been fighting. Fighting for what I love, what I want and what I believe in. Leaving high school, Tash and I have not had the smoothest of rides as I moved on to university with Renae, a friend I met at 6th form, and she went on to Teacher's college. We both went on to face our separate battles. It was rough but not so noticeably since school was particularly good at distracting us. We had our shares of meltdowns and even called an end to our friendship for three long months. KK had no idea that went down to this very day.

As the days turned into weeks and weeks turned into months, I kept asking myself where I went wrong. I could not help but reminisce on the memories we shared. Why be so bothered you may ask? Do not you have Renae? It was not so easy as said. Renae and I shared a different but nonetheless remarkably close bond. It is not easy to get over almost 8 years of friendship just like that.

I walked about a mile and a half every day from my house of boarding to my university and back. This specific afternoon I was just so out of it. I came home, dropped my bag and lay in bed. My phone vibrates, I ignored it. It vibrates once more, and I picked it up just because I do not want to have my parents worried about trying to get to me. Well, it was not my parents, it was my best friend.

I felt butterflies in my stomachs, even before reading the first sentence. I probably took friendship too seriously, but when I care for someone, I give it all I got. And as a result, when I hurt, it hurts bad. I will spare you all the details of what the text messages entailed, just know that was our first and last fight. We do not always agree on the same stuff, but wisdom comes with maturity, thank God for that.

Ever Since then we have been one hundred percent each other's biggest fan. Got a new job? We celebrate together. Having a baby? We celebrate together. Graduation? You name it. Every moment in our lives we have celebrated together, even when we were separated by thousands of miles apart.

I was more than honored to have KK being my Maid of Honor in 2018 while on the other hand heartbroken that Tash could not make it to the United States for it. It was a bittersweet feeling, knowing that they will be cheering me on one of the biggest days of my life and a day where I most definitely needed them the most. To this very day our friendship is one that I will forever cherish and one that a lot imitates. "Anything is possible when you have the right people there to support you" Misty Copeland.

Chapter Four

IF ONLY I KNEW

Grow up and be a good girl they say. Be a doctor, a lawyer whatever you may. Growing up by itself took so much from me, countless meltdowns. I did not know much but what I knew was that I did not want high school to be my final schooling destination. I heard my classmates talk about college and university, but I know for me that was a long shot. Not only I was still undecided on what I wanted to be, but my family would not be financially able to support me.

Being the determined person I am, I applied to three universities to study Registered nurse. My family had no clue. I did everything online and even applied for student loans. One afternoon I walked by the post office to collect our monthly electricity bill as usual. The Postmistress handed it to me, I politely said thank you and walked away. I did not even make it three steps away before she called me back saying I got two mails for myself. I was confused as to why I am receiving mails, not remembering that I had applied to colleges and universities.

I took the mail and held them close to my Chest. I felt as though I needed to use the bathroom, like really use the bathroom if you know what I mean. I started sweating and contemplating. Should I open them now? What if I did not get in? How am I going to take them home? Will my parents still be proud of me? Countless questions flooding my mind.

I gave up. I finally stop resisting the urge to open them. I was halfway home. I sat at a little ten feet bridge on a piece of log. I opened the first one, which was addressed from one of the top nursing schools in Jamaica and the Caribbean. I jumped up and screamed in joy for being accepted. After reading the first letter, I had a sense of relief. I was like, "How bad can it get from here". Pretty bad, since the first college that accepted me is known for its ridiculously high tuition fees.

I shoved the ripped enveloped and open letter into my pocket and proceeded to the next. I alighted from the log the second time and fell to my knees. This second acceptance was from my number one pick of university that I want to attend, The University of the West Indies, Mona. I picked up the letter out of the rubbles, shook the dust off and reread just to reassure myself that it is not all in my head.

It was not in my head. I was reading correctly. I took the time to read the entirety of the letter only to stumble upon a hard reality. I was most definitely accepted to the university but not for a Registered nurse. I was accepted to do a bachelor's degree in Public Policy and Management. First things first, I have never heard of that before, thus as a result I have no idea what it entailed.

I did not let it bother me as I have one more letter to open. And just like that I was accepted for nursing at another prestigious university. I quickly gathered all the scraps of papers, crunched them between my palms and pushed them as far as I can inside of my pockets. My heart raced so fast. I start thinking about how I am going to approach my parents or whether I should tell them or not.

I was now about eight minutes walk away from my house. I started walking extra fast, it took me three minutes to get home. I literally sped half the way home. Here I am now sitting on my house steps, breathing short and heavy. My dad came on the veranda immediately and asked if I am ok and who was chasing me. I quietly muttered, "I'm ok, I just walked way too fast".

Around five minutes has passed, and I am still sitting there. My mom was at the back cooking outside. She smelled like burned pimento wood. In her hand she held a kitchen towel and a spoon. "You just come back from the post office, or a long time you reach back?" she said. "No mam, I came back about five minutes ago" I replied. "Oh, true you just sit down deh so" she continued.

"You get the light bill?", she asked. "Yes mam" I replied as I tried to be careful of giving her one of my letters instead. My heart pounds as I reach to get her the electricity bill. In all honesty, I know my parents would be proud to know that I got accepted into three different colleges, I was simply scared because I did not want them to feel pressured knowing they weren't in the position financially to help me.

I just could not keep it all to myself, so I called my dad in the room to tell them the good news. I started out by unfolding those severely crushed letters and reading them aloud to my parents. At the end of my last letter my dad said, "dem sound good, but weh we ago get d money from fi you go?" our eyes met in the middle. I started to get emotional, and I remember my mom saying not to cry, God will provide a way if I must go.

I did not have one of those celebratory college sendoff parties, because I was still unsure if I was going to be able to attend. It was early summer, so it is kind of gives us some wiggle room to talk about it as a family. A family member suggested a student loan to me. At first my parents were a little skeptical. They then gave me the permission to apply, and I did just that and used my two elder sisters as my guarantor for the first year.

Do you know how they say there is a good in every tough situation? Well, that summer I was going to experience it firsthand. If you would recall in my earlier chapters, I mentioned how the church is all our family knew, I was raised in the church, and was also broken by the church. That summer is still to date the worst summer of my life. There was some misunderstanding and miscommunication between my leaders and I which transpired into a nightmare.

Remember how I mentioned that my mom does not let us go anywhere away from school or church? Well, that summer was so bad she sent me away to one of my elder sisters to stay for a while. On second thought, my siblings are out of the no-go zone. We are always allowed to go to their houses, but it was my first time staying for an extended period.

A month has passed, and I was still there with my sister. I was starting to get comfortable with my new normal. I enjoyed going to church and not having to listen to a whole sermon centered around how disrespectful young people are. It was a good feeling, and I sure could get used to it. And even though things have been resolved and I have an incredibly good relationship with all involved at the time, that specific point in time was my main driving force to what was going to happen next.

One day as I woke up to start my chores, my phone rang. It was my mom. She told me good morning as always and asked how I was feeling. My mental health was particularly important to my family as they all knew I took the situation hard and that I did not deserve the treatment I received. I sat down on my sister's veranda to be a little more comfortable while on the call. "Which college did you say accepted you again?" my mommy asked. And I replied. She further went on to ask me which one I am going to choose, and I told her The University of the West Indies, Mona. I answered without even second guessing how we were going to afford it. She said,

"Have you replied to them yet?", I said no! She said, "Reply to them that you will be coming September.

My heart dropped. I said, "how are we going to afford it mom? Are you sure about this?" she said, "yes, I am very sure, God is going to make a way for you my child, enough is just enough. You already applied for a student loan. I have a strong feeling you will get it. It would be best for you to go to college than to come back to this drama" I could not believe what I just heard. To hear my mom, say all that I could tell she was hurt and just had about enough of everything.

Finding a house in Kingston close to a college or university for commuting can be difficult as they are usually expensive and filled up fast. I did not know that you should go house searching months before school begins unless you can afford living on campus. I did not have the luxury of doing that since my decision to attend university was last minute. I knew God had this all planned out for me when he sent Shanieka Bryan, a friend and classmate in High school to my rescue.

One week before my orientation, I received a call from Shanieka about needing a roommate. That was the quickest yes, I have said in my life. I did not know the location, I did not ask about the cost, I just knew that I was going. I rushed to my mom to tell her the news. She was happy that I got a room but sad that she could not afford it. Shanieka did tell me how nice the property owner was and recommended that I give her a call about my financial trouble.

My mom and I got to it immediately and got her on the first ring. We introduced ourselves and just cut straight to the chase. My mom was able to convince her that she could be trusted, and we will pay our debt in a timely manner. She agreed to our terms and conditions and said I could move in whenever I want.

On Saturday August 23, 2014, I hugged my parents and siblings as I walked out of the house with a huge purple suitcase and a brown travel bag on top and my knapsack over my back. I had no idea how my first night in Kingston was going to be. But what I knew was that whatever may come my way God was going to pull me through and I was going to make the best of every bad dire situation.

I arrived at my destination around 5 Pm. I was tired and exhausted as I haul my belongings for more than half of a mile. I laid on the side of the room which was assigned to me by my roommate. That is just how it worked when you were not the first person to choose what you want. I was ok with it. Was rather grateful that I did not have nowhere to stay.

Did you know that when you are starting university you should bring pots and pans, bath pans, iron, fans etc.? My roommate had all those things and there I was with just clothes and hygiene products. I could not help but feel as though I was starting to fail already. I took the Sunday to rest and get to know the rest of my housemates as the following Monday I was going to start my orientation. My orientation went through to Thursday giving us an early weekend.

I did not hesitate. I went straight to Clarendon, which took roughly 2 hours. I was so happy to see my family. It felt as though I have been gone for quite some time. The first thing I noticed was that there was a feed bag filled with oranges, yam, plantains, sugar cane, among others. My God father, Langy" who is a farmer and father to me brought it there because he knew I was coming home for the weekend. Close to it was another with similar stuff inside that my dad packed for me.

I was overwhelmed with joy to see that my family was preparing for me. My mom gave me a brand-new pot set she received for Mother's Day. It was so hard for me to accept it, but she insisted. Every piece of clothing that I brought to Kingston was given to me by my sister Kay, she stripped her closet clean to make sure I have clothes to wear to school. I went back to Kingston with everything for my comfort. Every one of my siblings that was living on their own at the time gave me something from their household. I went to Kingston feeling loved and whole.

First year was very rough, from loud housemates on their video games to not being able to come up with the rent on the due date. Even though I was given the opportunity to pay it when I could, I could not help but feel ashamed every morning when I walked past my landlady's house to go to school and back. I felt helpless. One Monday morning I woke up saying to myself enough is enough I will have to get a Job at school to help back my parents up financially.

I used one whole week in school filling out job applications. I was desperate. I really did not care what the job description was. I got discouraged so many times because of hearing students speak of how hard it is to get a job on the school campus. I stopped thinking about it too much, but still thinks about it, nonetheless. Out of nowhere I got a call to work as a student courtesy officer, I was so happy that I cried. I called my parents to tell them the news and I could feel a sense of burden just lifted off their shoulders. It was a game changer, a blessing and a curse.

My first paycheck was exactly Two Thousand Two Hundred and Fifty Dollars. Equivalent of US Twenty to Twenty-Three dollars based on the value of the dollar. With that money I was able to pay my electricity bill, my internet bill, buy a little grocery and have a little pocket change. It was not enough for a month's rent, but it at least took a couple expenses off my parents. My month's rent at the time was Eight Thousand dollars (JMD) equivalent to US Seventy-Five Dollars.

As the months went by, I would continue to fill the gap for those small expenses while my parents and siblings worked together to pay my rent. My mom has been a diligent worker all her life. She has done some very strenuous tasks to provide for us. Around age 50 she stopped working so hard and started resting more as she began to feel the pain of her younger years.

Watching us struggle as a family to send me through university really took a toll on her. That was when she decided to go to Ocho Rios to do a "live in job" taking care of an old lady.

Quite frankly I was not happy with her decision, but I could understand why. I could not help but feel guilty, that I am causing my mother who has been experiencing ache and pain to do more work for me. She explained to me that she will be fine as all she is required to do is make meals and minimal house cleaning. That did give me a sense of relief. My mom makes Five hundred Dollars more than the cost of my rent every two weeks. It was a huge sacrifice, but she made it happen, now I was able to pay my rent on time. My faith in God has always been strong or so I Thought as it is soon to be put to test. Will I remember that I had served an on time, omnipresent God.

Chapter Five

ALL IS NOT LOST

So, do you know how they always say, behind a frowning providence, there hides a smiling face? Well, for months I could not find my smiling face. I was down to almost just bones after waves and waves of depression. I was never known to have a huge body mass index (BMI). The most I weighed then was 120 pounds. And I did love it. But just imagined me weighing just 90 pounds. I have asked God for job opportunities, and he came through for me. However, take it from me, never ask God for a blessing you are not prepared for, and I will tell you why.

Ever wanted to buy a nice couch for your living room but have nowhere to put it? Because an old one that your great grandma gave to you is sitting in the space. It is shredding its fabric, it is broken, it is just ugly. But every day you walked past it, you looked at it because great grandma gave it to you, so you are trying to honor it. It is good to honor, but there must be a breaking point.

Just like that every day I told God I need a Job without wondering how the work hours going to interfere with my class hours. Will I be able to be home in time to get assignments done? Are there any extra resources that this job is going to require of me to acquire? How bad will this Job complicate my everyday life? These were some of the questions I should have answered before asking God to provide me with a Job. Am I being ungrateful for such a provision? No, I am not. What I am doing is acknowledging some of my mishaps of not making the best of what God has given to me and ending up failing severely.

After I received the Job, things were sailing smoothly financially. That was a tremendous feeling knowing that I do not have to worry about it anymore. I felt at peace with myself and started to get comfortable. My focus was now drifted from getting good grades to getting more work hours. For that job, we had the choice of choosing our available hours. I think that was convenient as I already knew that I would be using my free hours in between classes to work.

My first week was not so good as I did not get many hours as other workers hours clashed with mine for the same post. This happened for about a week, and I just grew tired of the situation. The following weekend it was time to submit our available hours. I grabbed my subject timetable and carefully browsed through it. After I was finished, I ended up with the same six available hours. Things were not looking good for me.

I remember grabbing my timetable and starting to categorize my subjects from especially important to not so important, making sure to have my tutorials as particularly important, since we get grades for attendance and participation. As I browsed through my lectures, I started thinking, "oh, we are going to get the notes for these anyways" and just like that I got an extra two hours of work because I would not be attending that class. For that week I have in total 18 work hours.

At the time I was happy, started calculating my paycheck for the next two weeks and all the things I will be able to do and buy. I called my mom to tell her that I got some extra hours that week and she reminded me to not let the work hours interfere with my class time and I promised her I would not. I lied and I am not proud. Deep down it hurts, but all I wanted to do was to start earning enough to have them not worried about me and I went about it the wrong way.

I started missing months and months of lecture classes. I would be lost every time I showed up at tutorial class. Questions were asked that I could not answer. I would normally have to ask a classmate what chapters we are now at the time. I was at a total loss and my tutors were starting to notice that something was not right. Not only was I not attending the lecture classes, but I was also not reading the same lecture notes that were posted on my portal.

I got caught up in overtime, extra hours, on call just to make more money while my body, mind and soul was deteriorating. For one I could not read the notes after the lecture hour had passed because I was still working. Secondly, I clean, do my laundry, pick up groceries and comb my hair on Saturdays and go to church on Sundays. Somedays I got home so late I just completely passed out from exhaustion. I would wake up the next morning with a not so good odor, still in my work uniform.

My roommate would check in on me every now and then to see how I was doing, because of how drained I used to be. She shared dinner with me and just helped in whatever ways she could loan herself to me at the time. It was a nice feeling to know that someone recognized my fight to be a better person but was just having a bad moment and was there to support.

One of the sad realities is that the first thing I did after waking up in the mornings is check my phone. Not praying, not checking in with my parents or friends, just straight social media platforms. I am not proud of it, but it is what it is. One morning after checking all those apps I noticed I had two messages in my university's email. I was very hesitant to read them because I was never notified of anything school related.

On second thought how bad can it be? Well, that morning was bad. Simply put, I was asked to withdraw from the faculty below my Grade Point Average (GPA) fell below 2.00, the acceptable average. Considering that this was at the end of the second semester in year one I was devastated.

How could this be, my journey had just begun. I have my dream chart hanging in my dorm room, all the goals I wanted to achieve within the next three years. Is all this over already? I just started. How am I going to tell my family about this? Better yet, what am I going to tell my family? That I was not disciplined enough, I was not able to finish? How am I going to go back to my community? People already did not want me to succeed. Shall I give them glory over me? I think not.

I sat in my room and had my fair share of sorrows. My roommate was not there so that gave me a little more privacy to cry out all my pain. I felt my chest tightened up with a pain I've never felt before. It was awful. I sat up and leaned my back against the frame of my bed and stared straight into a three feet mirror attached to the wall. I looked straight at myself and said these words of affirmation, "you are strong, you are capable, you are not a failure, you are a fighter, this too shall pass, you will overcome. Your past does not determine your future, you are God's chosen vessel, all is not lost!"

Hearing those words coming out of my mouth was not shocking in the least. I lived by those mantras. I have always had a brighter look at life, there is always a way out. I took a grain of salt with every dire situation. I am no stranger to prayer and the works of God. I have seen him come through for me on countless occasions and without a doubt I know this situation was not an exception.

I wiped my tears and stood upright. I grabbed my washcloth, my toothbrush and toothpaste and headed straight to the shower. I came out and got dressed like I was not crying an hour ago. That day I did not have any class until 1PM and thank goodness I was not scheduled for work either. I shut the gate behind me after leaving home around 9:30 AM. "Good morning singer, you are looking so splendid today" a passerby said. Out of respect I replied, "thank you, I appreciate it" he had no idea the pain I was feeling on the inside and I am glad I did not portray an attitude to make a stranger think otherwise. People living in the area that I was staying for school call me "singer" because that's all I do on the weekends when cleaning and just going about my business.

It was 10 AM on the dot when I walked into the Campus Registrar's office. Three students were ahead of me waiting to speak to an official as to why they were failing, just like myself. I could not help no noticed the shaking legs, the biting of the nails and the runny eyes. I thought to myself, why am I so relaxed? Am I not taking this seriously? Then a voice in my head said, "the battle is not yours" and that was my confirmation to know that God was going to take me through.

I start hearing the students planning on reciting what they were going to tell the officials. I looked up to the ceiling and said, "God, fill my mouth with words that you want me to say" and just started crying. I came into the office with the most confidence and got distracted by what someone else was doing and started losing my faith in God. At the time, I did not think I was failing God because all I could think about is the fact that my reason for failing would not be enough to save me. But trust me I was. I started doubting him even after asking him to direct my words.

It was now my time to see the officials. I composed myself and walked into the office humble yet confident. The broad questions like, what do you think are causing you to fail? What is going on in your life? Was not asked to me. She looked me dead in the eye and said I only have one question for you, "why is your best was not good enough?" I broke down in tears. It felt like someone put a dagger to my heart. I looked straight back at her with tears running down my face and said, "you had no idea what I am going through, I have had my fair share of pain and just when I thought I was going to get healing you tore my heart wide open, thank you"

I started getting up out of the chair and was about to walk out of that office, that school for good. I did not even make three full steps before she summoned me to sit down and explain what is going on. As a starter I started telling her a little bit about my background and life growing up. I shared the struggle of not paying my rent and finding food. I did not make it through my statement before she broke down in tears. She looked at me and said, "you are a fighter, and you deserve a second choice, just please do not let me regret my decision"

I was overwhelmed with joy to hear her say those words. That day I told her I will not disappoint her. I felt relieved. I did not have to worry about telling my family about it anymore. It was almost time for my first class of the day, I was one of the first students present. I was always on time for my classes, but this was a massive wake up call. I realized the things we took for granted are always the things that came back to hurt us.

I get home that day and send in my letter of resignation from my job for the entirety of the following year. I made a promise to my campus registrars and to myself that I will not fail, and I was not going to risk a second choice such as this one. That following year I got back on top of my game in my academics. I did not fail a single subject in year two. I fight because above making my parents and family proud I want to make myself proud. I have always done things "for me", not what my parents want but what I want. And as a result, what I wanted has always been what my parents wanted too so it makes me even more happy to accomplish such goals.

Hebrews 11:1-2, "Now faith is the substance of things hoped for, the evidence of things not seen. For by it the elders obtained a good report" throughout that phase of my life, I have seen where my faith was put to the test and on countless occasions I failed. Doubt will overrule your faith, and as humans it is easier for us to doubt than trust the process and trust God that he will show up and show out for us. I am a living testimony that he never goes back on his words and his promises are true.

Therefore, I encourage you today, not to lose hope. God is never slack concerning his promises. He may be four days late, but he will be on time. Who said it was going to be easy? But it will for sure be worth it. You are going to want to give up and give in and that is natural. But if you can muster up just a little bit of strength to go on, you will be happy you did not throw it all in. Trust the timing. Trust the process.

Chapter Six

RESPECT THE STRUGGLE

" **S**uccess is not final; failure is not fatal. It is the courage to continue that counts" Winston Churchill. This quote has always been a part of my life. It takes a lot to not feel as if you are dying mentally, physically or emotionally after every failure. Whether you feel as if you are failing as a parent, a student or a friend, failure just always leaves a very unpleasant aftertaste to your soul and a heavy heart.

As someone who had their fair share of struggles, I was determined to not walk along a certain path ever again under no circumstances. For some, respect for the struggle may mean something different from what it means to me. I have come to understand that life has a way of humbling us, and for me it is through my struggles. For every failed opportunity like not getting the promotion at work, a loan was not approved, or your credit score was too low to get a mortgage.

Why should I respect the struggle? I am going to prove that I ruled my own destiny. I am a fighter; I will never quit. No matter what happens, seven timeless fall seven times rise. That was my mindset after every disappointment in my life. The only respect I had for my struggle was talking to it. "Ok, I know you are capable of taking me from a hundred to zero in split seconds. I identify your existence and your capabilities. You knocked me to my knee's countless times, but I will not stop trying. I served an all-present God. It is either you or me and I am not planning on giving up anytime soon".

Pretty crazy right? Like whom talks to someone or something they cannot, see? I do. I served a God who has proven to be mighty in power, all powerful and omnipresent. I was not sure what force it was but by faith I placed it under subjection through Christ Jesus. I respect my struggle enough to have a conversion with it.

Struggle does not respect you because of how ambitious you are, how financially stable you are or how gorgeous you look. As humans we all have different struggles. What might be a struggle for me may have you thinking, 'like seriously'. Let me just say this, we do not need to be judged because our struggles vary. We need to start embracing each other through their struggles and understanding from their standpoint.

Struggles does not require patience and the "things will get better "mindset. You must be cold, brutal and just final with it. You cannot let platitude control your life; you will never win. Many years in property have taught me that. I never respect my struggles. All I knew was that I hate not having things to my disposal, such as eating whatever I want whenever I want, going to the ice cream shop on Sundays or choose which outfit I want to wear or not. I did not have that luxury. I went head on with the struggles that presents themselves to me and my family. No food in the house? Early Saturday morning we would head out to the river as it was our main source of games and proteins. We do bird hunting too but not as regular as we fish. If it lives in the river then it is edible with a few exceptions of frogs and snails. Fish, shrimp, crawfish, eels etc. we would just spend the entirety of the day forging for food of any kind while assisting ourselves to people's fruits such as sugar canes, oranges and mangoes along the riverbed.

The breadfruit trees that lined the riverbanks would be our next task after fishing. Now that we would have obtained our protein it was time to source some starch. My brothers would them climbed the breadfruit trees and handpicked every one of them. To prevent bruising, they would drop them it the water and we would swim for them as they float. After this, we would be on our way with anywhere from twenty to twenty-five breadfruits. Some fit for boiling and the rest for roasting. And let us not forget those buttery ackee trees on our way home. This goes perfectly with some roasted breadfruit. No, they are not on our property, but where I grew up everybody's property is for everybody; with a few exceptions of persons who really don't get along with the entire community and as such the community doesn't go their way either.

I saw struggle firsthand and up close, and I hated it. And my first instinct said, 'run Sher'. It makes you look for anyway out. It does not make you question the percussions or consequences that may follow. It makes you do stupid things. But on second thought, I said to myself. I will fight to the death of me than running from something that I have control over. It makes me angry. Not with myself or my family but with its existence and presence in my life. And though you cannot see it in the literal world to give it a slap across its face I see it in everything that I did. Going to school without lunch, washing and wearing the only two underwear that I owned and sleeping on a 10-year-old sponge with a sister and a cousin. It was just everywhere.

I just wanted to be at a place mentally, emotionally, and physically where I was not tired. Tired of never winning, tired of hoping for better days to be in a better place where the floors were not as the same as outside. Hoping to wake up and be confused at what I wanted for breakfast because I have too many options. Hoping that this life was just about to be over with and the best years of our lives was yet to come. Lord knows, I hope. I went to bed at nights and fantasize on the finer things in life, praying to God that one day he might deliver us from such extreme property; and high hopes that by some miracle or so coincidence I wasn't going to wake up in that same space physically or mentally.

I got tired of hoping but have not giving up trying to escape. I was so through and brutal with our struggles that sometimes I think I turned away people who genuinely care and wants to help. That right there was the problem. I could not see past that has been pitied and sorry for. I want for once to be the other person on this side of life. I want to be the giver. For too long people always wants to help, weather I accept or not, there is always someone offering. And while you may see this as thoughtful and kind, many did it so they could tell someone else that they helped you. Not because their heart is in the right place. From kids sharing their meals at schools to people giving my mom clothes, I was just about done with every bit of those handouts.

Perfect example, there was this lady at our church that was good friends other my family. She was a dressmaker. She is always dressed nicely. Of course, it is expected. She is a dressmaker after all. One Sunday, I saw her giving my mom a bag. I could not see what exact was in it, but I could tell it was containing cloth material. I was a decent size to say the least. Well, as a child, I have no authority in questioning my elders or what we called "putting my nose in places it does not belong", so I quickly forget about it as I moved around in greeting the brethren's before heading home.

This same afternoon we got home, my mom called my bigger sister Roxann, my cousin Jody and myself into her bedroom. You guessed it, there was the same bag I saw in church. We all started at each other than at the bag and back and forth without saying a word. Well, at least not for long. I could not keep quiet. "Mommy where you get this from?" I asked. Knowing my mom, she is going to tell me, "A nuh everything pickney must know". To my pleasant surprise, she told us all the details. Say what now? We were all shocked. Shocked for many reasons. For one, my mom never accepts anything from people for her kids and two, and if by any chance she took something from someone she trusts she never tells us. So, yes, it all took us by surprise. Before you know it, we are digging through the bag to see what we like, or should I say I was? My sister and my cousin were not thrilled about it at all. And even though none of us has a lot of clothes to wear in general, I was the only one acting desperate and happy.

While I was knee deep in the bag, I heard my sister said, "mi no want nobody sorry fi me" followed by my cousin saying, "A wear and left dem wah come give we, after we are not worse off than anybody else" hissed her teeth and walk away. For some reason I was not phased on but, I dig deeper. "Ooh I like this one, nah too ugly" throwing and tossing clothes everywhere. At that point in time, I did not see a problem, I saw a solution. Sherrian has a shortage in clothes, Sherrian was given a ton of clothes, problem solved. Simple. But what I could not get over was the fact that my mom told us all the details of this bag.

Knowing how I am I could not let it slide, so I asked my mom. "Mom why makes you tell us who gave it to you this time?" She said, "The thing is, you are not so little anymore. You might even recognize some of these clothes so I told you who gave them to me so you can decide if you want to wear them or not". After this response I could not help but think, wow! My mom is really seeing us as young adults with some amount of control over our lives. I said this because, if you were raised in the Jamaican culture, you would understand that being sixteen, eighteen or thirty-five doesn't mean anything to your parents if you are still under their roof. I was just in the tenth grade, so that was important for me.

These bags of clothes would show up at our house every now and then and I was just about tired of them. I remember looking at the last bag that came home with so much scorn and bitterness. My mom was confused. Why was I not going through it like previous times? I was just through with taking handouts from people. I did not care what was their intentions behind it, I was just through.

I remember my cousin Jody walking in and see the bag. The looked on her face says get this bag out of here. Not before long she said to my mom, "this is the last one coming here, don't take not one more from anybody, we better than this". And that my friends were the last bag of clothing ever made it to our house. Unlike the last time, every word she said connects with me and I could not agree with her anymore. My mom was very understanding and realized that the choices and decisions that were made were totally justified since they only affect us and not her.

I am still not sure how my mom breaks the news to her about not wanting any more bags of clothing from her, or where the ones we already had went but what I'm sure about is that, that part of our lives was over with, and we did not have to feel bad for doing what we did. God has a way of turning things around and thankfully the worst years of our lives was coming to end. Or that is what we thought.

You know how they say nothing lasts forever and only a good salvation will last! Well, sorry to burst your bubble but some struggles do last forever IF you chose not to fix it. You cannot just sit at ease hoping for a change with not putting in the work. Work without faith is dead just as much as faith without work. To receive any good result, it takes persistence, and a lot of it. It is not something you sit and daydream about, it acts.

Unbelievably everyone was born with their own unique purpose. For some they just know what their purpose is and pursue it, unlike others they struggle with identifying what is their purpose. As a result of this, it results in poor relationship choices, staying at a job you really hate or wasting four years of your life at a university doing a career you barely like. I know this because I have spent my university years majoring in a major of which I do not even have a clue of where I could work with such a degree. And even though it turned out okay for me on the one hand that I have grown to have a passion for such field it can be stressful, nonetheless.

It is our responsibility to never give up on that dream, passion or urge to do something your heart truly desire. Fear and doubts will be inevitable, but it is the determination and hunger for success that will drive you to the peak of greatness. Self-assessment is particularly important. One should know what they really want. What makes your eyes sparkle with delight whenever you speak about all the things you want to achieve? What is the first step you will take in ensuring that you are on a solid path? Who do I want to take on this journey with me? Am I surrounded by the right set of people? These are some of the questions you should ask yourself before proceeding.

After getting everything into place, the reality of all the decisions made will be in full effect. You will want to quit, that will be the first thing that will come to mind. That little inner voice you should never listen to, not when you are on the verge of becoming who you are destined to be. Unfortunately, some of us made the decision to listen to that voice which leads to failure. No, failure was not an option but not having enough courage or support often creates a blank path. It is important to be surrounded by people who will encourage you to go on, no matter how much you want to give up.

I was blessed to be born into a family with parents and siblings who supports me all the way. They comfort, console and gives constructive criticism when necessary. I have never taken for gratitude their genuine support and help throughout my life; however, I was not always grateful. At that phase in my life, I did not understand how important it is to have family that supports you. There are a lot of people who had to confide in strangers and keep meeting new people to share things with because they are a part of a distant family. Just never take for granted the people who wants to genuinely see you win.

Growing up I heard life is what you make it, but that could not be any further from the truth. Had it been that I had given up all those times when life knocks me to my feet, I would not have been where I am today. What if I had said, "well, this is life I will just have to understand that university is not for everyone". Life to me is constant work, growth and changes. It cannot be confined, and everyone has their own unique share of it. A lot of times we tend to get confused by what other people have going on in their lives, thinking it is the ideal lifestyle. If you remember earlier on in the second chapter, you would have recall me mentioning that kids in primary school use to buy my homemade lunch from me. To me, I thought having the money to buy whatever I want was the ideal thing at the time. I was wrong. What was ideal was enjoying a good healthy meal, which I was blessed to have but did not realize it at the time.

People create all these socially structured timelines on their lives and then get angry with the world and themselves when it does not work out. I get it. It is understandable to set goals and work towards them. What is not okay is to have someone setting those goals for you and pressure you to reach them despite of. That my friend is not acceptable. Life has its benefits and its mishaps, and that is what makes it so sophisticated and spontaneous. Nothing is never sure; things does not always goes as planned and plans fall through sometimes.

At around ten years old I started telling people when I grow up, I am going to be a bank manager. My mom being the supportive mother that she is, would always tell me yes, I can be that and whatever else I want to be. It was not before long that I change my mind and decided to be a lawyer instead. I would practice how I was going to defend my clients with my sisters. By the time I reach High School I now wanted to become a soldier, then a teacher then, a Chef and it continues like that until I was starting university. But through it all, my parents have never told me that I could not be any of the above-mentioned titles. They never forced a career on me and pressure me to peruse it for them. They understand that if my career choice makes me happy then they are happy for me.

There were so many things that I knew I wanted to achieve at a certain age, but I was not applying pressure to those thoughts and ideas, I just consistently work towards it. Some of which includes finishing college by age 23, getting married by age 24, having a baby by age 28 and buying a house by 30. So far all of these seems to be on track but was never rushed. It takes challenging work and consistency. But moreover, they were all on my time, my set goals and not another. And that is the most important thing.

I know a lot of people in this time who are struggling to keep their lives together for one reason or the other. They are mentally devastated because they are twenty -five and not owning a house, or thirty and not get a college degree. Social constructed laws like these affect the way you see yourself as a person. Many think they are failing because society paint a huge canvas of what you should be or what you should achieve at a certain time in your life and if you fail at such then you fail at life. That is a lie. It is okay to have you first child at thirty years old, it is okay to buy a house at fifty and starts university at twenty-six.

There has always been a stigma surrounding a female getting pregnant out of high school. "Oh my God, she just threw away her life", or "why she could not wait until after college?" I was blessed to have dodged that bullet, but many others cannot say the same. People looked at them with so much hate and scorn, I feel for them sometimes. Who really gets to decide how a person lives their life and what choices are classified as "the end of their lives"? no body other than that individual. But people these days have invested so much in businesses that have zero concerns about them and that is incredibly sad.

The worst part of those stories is that those people judging are no example. They themselves have their first child at fifteen years old, does not attain even a secondary education, does not have a job, but they have all the solutions to a problem that's not theirs, but just can't seems to fix one of their own. So, what if she gets pregnant in high school? Is it the end of the world? It is not. She can always go back and finish, then attend university. But, because of these socially constructed timelines people face a lot of pressure. Not only does this creates a timeline but it also creates a sequence.

You are supposed to finish high school, finish college, get married, have a nice career, have a nice house and car, have a baby then live happily ever after. And once again I was fortunate to have followed in that sequence but not many can relate. Forget this structure. Have your nice house, then have your baby, go to college, get married. There is no right and wrong way at life. Life is hard, it is complex and there is not just one way at taking it on. We ourselves are complex beings. So, the next time you think your life is not lining up with what your parents planned for you, or the picture society paints, remember this, your destiny and your future was not created by society or your parents and nothing you do will ever change what was destined for you.

What I have noticed growing up was that, having a baby and getting married were two of the biggest "fever catching" occurrences. After one person in the community or the church gets married, everybody wants to, well at least that is what I thought when I was younger. Well, growing up I understood better what was going on. No, it was not a "fever catching "thing. It was pressure of some sort or another. When people reach their mid-twenties the ideology that they should have their lives together start plaguing their minds. And if that was not enough to brought stress to their lives, some of them have parents, friends and in-laws to remind them every day that they are getting old and does not have a baby or getting old and not married as yet.

I have always heard the saying, "the struggle is real" but I just used it lightly when I did not get paid on time or when I could not afford that super expensive purse. But truth is, there are people out there who have it worse. Am I saying my experience is not a struggle? No, I am saying that there is someone out there who could use my help who are facing bigger struggles.

Everyone deals with struggles differently. Pressure and influence are two of the main struggles teenagers and young adults are faced with. Influence from your peers may vary from parental influences and pressure. Do not get great advice confused with pressure. Because quite often people do that. They ended up terminating friendships because a friend is "always trying to run their life", when that friend was just being true to them. And some individuals even cut ties with their parents because they are passed eighteen years old, and their mom is still "treating them like a child" by correcting them are having a conversation about their decisions. These are harsh realities. And even though there are controlling friends and parents, more than seventy percent are not like that based on statistical evidence. There is something about sex, marriage ad having a baby that I found out can be very pressuring.

Teenagers especially experienced a vast amount of peer pressure surrounding having a boyfriend sex. Everyone wants to experience it and if you are not doing it for varied reasons, the larger population of who are sexually active push a certain narrative unto you, creating the idea that you are missing life. I for one never experienced sexual pleasure until my early twenties which was too long for the majority. I have spent most of high school into university lying about my imaginary boyfriend Jamie, which lives in Canada.

I cannot tell you that I have experienced pressure from peers to get involved sexually, because I did not. My friends knew where I stand on such topic, plus they understand the biblical aspect as it relates to me being a part of the church. They did try setting me up with different boys to say the least. I have received a lot of pressure regarding relaxing my hair and wearing pants, but never about being involved sexually. And that is why it is important I chose the right people in your circle as I mentioned earlier.

On the contrary end family can be your worst nightmare sometimes. A lot of the struggles people faced are because family ignore their problem. But even then, there are two sides to every story, so let us start with the first one. Families ignores a relative struggle because that is their only option. I have seen relatives of mine disrespect their parents' family members by telling them to stay out of their lives, they have already done their jobs in raising them, they are a full-grown adult, and they don't need their parents anymore and things amongst those lines.

I am not a parent, but I cannot even bring myself to imagine how bitter that pill is to swallow, served by your own child. Sometimes all your intentions are pure and genuine. In situations like this a child puts themselves in a dire situation. No body, absolutely no one is ever going to have your back like your parents, especially your mother. I can't imagine life without my mom, and while I accept that one day all of us will have to go, I rather not think about it and live in the moment while appreciating every day that I get to hear her voice.

That same family member that I mentioned above, have faced bad verbal and physical abuse by her partner, some of which would be fatal if help was not close by. And by close by I mean her same family which she despises. She is one of those females who would rather supports and defends an abusive boyfriend than takes advice from a relative. She is so toxic to the point where she would run and cry to you about being in possible danger and then goes back to the boyfriend and told him you said she should break up with him. That was the most toxicity I've ever seen in my life.

On the other hand, families ignored you because they know if the help you, you are going to come out of the slum, out of the ghetto out of that small town and be great and do remarkable things. Yes, you heard me right. Families are one of the most jealous and most envious people you can have in your corner. They would rather to see you struggle every day and help you for that day. Anything more than that they will not volunteer.

They want to know that when they wake up the next morning you are still stuck in that small town. Not doing nothing new with your life, still begging for help from them and just the usual. I was very taken a back when I learnt of such cruelty, because all this time I was enjoying my supportive family not knowing what another family was going through. You would have thought strangers were the one stopping your blessings, it be your own blood sometimes. And even though I write it in words my mind still can't fathom such wickedness.

And while, yet another time I considered myself beyond blessed to not have experienced that, it is disturbing none the less to have seen a family member done such things and put another through hell.

So, remember earlier on I said one should not be judged based on what is considered or not considered a struggle, I still hold that sentiment. Struggles does presents themselves differently to everyone. And everyone coping mechanisms are different and unique. Survival is mandatory. One will ensure that they go to the extra mile to ensure that everyone around them have all the necessities required for their daily purpose. Some folks may think that average is okay. Being able to eat a daily meal each day is just above the poverty line. I strongly believe that everyone has a decision to make in regards of how they want to live their life within the next ten to twenty years.

That responsibility comes in your earlier years. During that time, you can set a solid foundation in building the type of life you want. It will not come easy, especially if you are not born with a 'gold spoon in your mouth'. Oh no, but it is your duty to lay out your plans and start the construction. Remember there is no one to be blamed if you end up somewhere, where there are only regrets and what ifs. Everything is in your hands. Be willing to take a step forward and risk it all. You will never know what it will be like until you give it a far try.

Struggles within itself is never a good thing but it for sure have a few perks. There are always lessons taught with each struggle. It always highlights your strengths and your weaknesses, and even discover strengths you did not know you had. Struggles often shows you who are bailing water out of your boat and who drilling holes. Who you can count on and who would rather see you fail? You get it. Simply put, struggles bring out the good and bad in people. One of the biggest weaknesses of knowing these benefits is that people tend to always go back where it hurts.

How could I be friends again with the person I considered a friend who watch and do nothing through my struggles. Who spread gossip to strangers about my struggles? Who makes shady post on social media about my struggles? I could not, but sadly a lot of people do not learn. While if you look on the other hand, it is not that they do not learn, it's that their surroundings are so toxic. The same people that spread gossip are the only person who would hang out with them or watch their kids while they run errands. It is like they are stuck, but truth is they are not.

They can move out of that little community where everybody knows everybody. It is always okay to start over. Meet new people, new friends, new school whatever it may. But as simply as it sounds to you, it is harder for the people in the situation. To them you are telling them to pack up everything and go, everything they have ever known to some place they are complete strangers. And if that was not enough, they are more than likely struggling financially already. Financial stability and independence is probably one of the biggest struggles known to humanity. This is not rocket science. We all love money. Some of my happiest days are when I do not have to worry how my bills re going to be paid. Money provides human with all the basics needs of life. And even when these are met, because of how complex we are basic will not do. We love the nice life. And nice life requires a lot of money. Go to college they say and get a degree then get you a respectable job. Well, so far, I have done that still cannot seems to get that opportunity. Some of the most financial unstable people I know are university graduates. The competition is so high, and not enough job provisions. As if struggling four years through university with hungry days, no textbooks, walking three miles every day and barely passing a course was not enough, well cheers to be back in your parents' house, eating their food, no job, student loan debt and can't contribute to anything. The system is cruel, and you must be a tough one to survive it.

No job wants to take you on because they are looking for "experienced individuals". How can that be when you are fresh out of university seeking experience in your field. This my friends are first class struggle. Infuriating is an understatement. It is disgusting, unfair, cold and not humane. How can we as a people escape such when we circulate the wealthy within the work force and ignore the poor and trying. The wealthy gets wealthier, and the poor get poorer. I still remember my first job that paid me eighteen thousand Jamaican dollar for three weeks, equivalence of one hundred and eighty US Dollars. I did not have any responsibility at the time other than finishing high school.

That day I receive the check, I could not stop smiling. I was able to pay my little sister's school fee, buy grocery for the house and give my parents a little pocket money which they use to send me back to school the following week. But the point I want to bring across is that having financial freedom is having power. Power to do whatever you want. Whenever you want. And while most of us continue to be patient, waiting on our breakthrough to have such independence the legal way, many others are forced to provide for themselves and their families illegally. And while it is socially unacceptable it is without debate that many of us can attest to such claims as wanting to be a part of that group but did not for one reason or the other.

Everyone has their own season. Some people might be ahead of you, that does not mean you are left behind. That is just their timing and God's plan. Be patient and wait on your season. Do not panic or worry, remarkable things are about to happen for you. When it is your time to start off in your rightful purpose, it is important to remain the same. Growth is a part of the process but grow humbly. Some people tend to forget this part most of the time. They begin to treat the ones who was always by their sides unfairly, their favorite word will be "I did not ask you to". Do not fall into that category. Grow. But never outgrow those who was always there for you.

Struggles are hard, they are ugly, and they are brutal. And the only way to overcome it is to return the same favor. Be cold, be brutal be harsh with it. You must be resilient and determine. It does not go away in one blow. It takes challenging work and dedication. And while your peers, your family and your friends may not respect your fight or just cannot understand why you are doing what you are doing, keep doing it. Keep pushing forward and never respect your struggles, respect God enough to know that he is willing and able to put your struggles behind you, for the last time.

Chapter Seven

TO HELL AND BACK

Many people share testimonials of some very dark days in their lives. They would outline the entire scenario from the cause, the experience and what pulled them through. Then at the end they would say, "I have been to hell and back" why did they say that? How bad a situation must be for you to use that phrase? Well, as bad as it makes you feel. For whatever reason they use it, it cannot be anything good. I have used that quote but for reasons like being presented with Satan himself. Satan for me was never the two-horn man with the two teeth and a metal fork as the picture depicts. It was in every man, woman, boy and girl that has ever caused me pain, harm, confusion and frustration. It was in every mouth that opened to speak ill of me. Every foot that trod to work iniquity against me. Every hand that set forth to poison the provision Christ Jesus have made for me. I was not able to see a physical depiction of Satan, but I have seen him every day in everyone that meant evil for my life.

They said keep your friends close but your enemies closer, and how ironic is it to have your enemy as a neighbor. Pretty close right! Well, it does not always work out to have them this close. Just for clarity, this neighbor is not a relative. I cannot remember the date exactly when it all started but I am quite sure of the year, 2009. I was in the 9th grade of school and my two eldest brothers were on their second and third years consecutively of the farm work program in Canada. The funny thing about this individual is that he was not always a stranger. He was a casual friend with my family, especially one of my eldest brothers. It is the type of friendship that speaks only about current events, politics and community event. No invitation to family events, no personal disclosure of life events. So basic neighborly affairs. My family have seen how he is with people he used to laugh with, so we had our guard up non the less. For the record I will be addressing this person as Satan because that is all he really was.

Two things I could not understand about people are, someone hating us for no reason and secondly hating us because we were coming out of extreme property. Like what demonic powers are you influenced by to be like that. How does watching an entire family suffer brings you relief or pleasure? After my brothers have been traveling for some time, the eldest decided to buy a car. Do you mean the same poor boy from down the lane? Yes, that same one. While we are happy that the tables were turning, Satan did not like that. Satan our neighbor. I still remember the first morning I woke up to loud, vulgar chattering. Everyone woke up confused trying to figure out what was going on, till at last my mother's name was mentioned. How is that possible though? My mom does not even have friends. What did my mother do this man now? Nothing. All I heard was "Norma and him pickney dem anuh no body, a mi first buys car and travel go foreign bout yah".

After hearing this my heart skipped a beat and my adrenaline rush hits and I remember running off the veranda picking up a rock to throw at him and my mom screamed, "Sher don't do it, use unuh head. A trouble him wah put unuh in. He knows if he pushed you enough you are going to attack him then he can get his glory of seeing you behind bars" I was halfway there when I heard my mom said this, and all I did was stand there and stared at Satan, dead in the eyes. I looked at him with so much anger, hatred and bitterness. I dropped the rock, while still steering at him for around five more minutes nonstop. Apart from the day that I lost my two cousins in a fire, I have never witnessed so much physical pain to my heart. It was as if my heart was coming out of my chest.

Did this man really go to his bed thinking about why our family was not dirt poor anymore? It must be for him to wake up that morning and decided to start on us. Just to clarify this man was our neighbor only because he had recently bought some pigs and put them on his family's land which share fence with us. So, his family lives there not him. So, he must be real trouble to come all the way there to start an argument with my family. Not one of my family members gave him the time of day. All my mother asked was what have she and her kids ever done to him. He could not answer as he continues to brag about how much he was the one who owned the first car, which is a lie. I am not sure if he planned the days and time when to argue with my family but for some reason there are never any males home. My dad or my brothers. These arguments would continue almost once every month.

God has blessed one of my big sisters with a job position in a government organization that a lot of people envied. It is not easy to not notice my sister in this organization when it is one of the biggest facilities that caters to everything official or governmental. So, of course he went there and saw my sister. He smiled, congratulated her and even have a little chit chat. To our surprise, around two weeks after that charming event, Satan presents himself again. He mentioned that "even john crow working in high places now" referring to my sister as a crow. How rude! I could not keep my mouth shut this time. I start answering him. It was head-to-head with us because I was not giving up and neither was Satan. My mom was in the back pleading for me to stop argue with him, but I had all that hurt built up inside of me from the previous time, so I just wanted to get it out. Out of respect for my mom, I stopped responding and so did he. It was without delay I realized that his goal is to push us to our limits. With me not responding to him, he did not have anything to feed his arguments off.

Remember those pigs I mentioned earlier? They gave us a very rough time. Having pigs squealing in your ears twenty-four seven is one thing. But having to put up with the unpleasant odor was a different type of stress. There were days when my family could not cook because of the odor. Or if we pushed through and cook, we could not eat our meals. It was as if you are eating pig feces, literally. It was gross, it was unpleasant, it was disgusting. I remember my mom talking to one of his relatives about the situation and it stir up another hell like argument. He may have mentioned it to Satan and oh he went off on my family again.

He told us how much we are bad hearted because we do not want him to strive. Excuse me! How is it that me telling him that eager his livestock ten feet away from my bedroom window is not wanting him to strive? Our health and overall well-being were at risk here, but that does not seem to concern him. Very alarming to say the least. It is common sense to know that and respect for those around you. But sadly, he did not possess any of those qualities. He was cruel, evil and mean. People like those can be hard to deal it.

The word of God taught us not to repay evil with evil and as such we did not return the favor to him. Anyway, you cannot be a coward with people like that. You must be fierce, upfront and final with them or else they will take every opportunity they get to abuse you mentally, cause honestly that is all he can do and is about. He is the biggest coward I have ever came across. There was this one time he gets into a physical fight with someone and all he did was stand behind his family hoping that they do something. In a matter of minutes, it got physical. Rocks throwing, machete drawing and all these things. Where is he? I thought to myself. I can hear his voice but not able to locate him. To my surprise, he was hiding behind my mom. What? When did we start talking again? Behind the same woman you cussed couple weeks ago. I think not. My mom being the sweetheart she is, was there trying to defend him and make peace. In that moment all I wanted to do was dragged my mom and let the guy on the other side gave him a fine whoop. I was so angry that my mom was there saving him. My mom was not doing this because of his sake. She was doing it because as a Christian that is probably what Jesus would have done. After all, he said "Love your enemies, bless them that curse you, do good to them that hate you, and pray for them that despitefully use you; that ye may be the children of your Father which is in heaven".

As spiritual as I was at the time, that biblical reference never crossed my mind once. I saw an opportunity to return revenge and I was ready for it to be served, cold. But the word of God also says, "vengeance is mine, I will repay". It was after the occurrence that these scriptures came to mind, not in the moment. To be honest, I was so mad I didn't even remember I was a Christian. I want to cuss at him, I want to send him to some dark places beyond his parents' private places, but I couldn't out of respect for my parents not because I was a Christian.

After this incident I thought to myself, well, he is going to stop starting drama and problems with my family now that he knows we are not who he said we were plus we were the only one to save his sorry ass that day. I was so wrong; I speak too quickly. Early Sunday morning as I was bailing water from the drum outside to shower and get ready for church I heard "dutty John crow unuh" what?? What have we done to Satan now? It is Sunday morning and as usual our music is shaking our roof, but it was a little bit too early to turn it on when I was bailing the water. As he continued to argue about how much he is a fighter and did not need any help I went in and turn on the music tuning him out, and just like that he shut up. He knows he will not be able to speak above the stereo, so he fed his pigs and went his way.

As time goes by, he finds new things to argue with us about. This would go by for years. We had just about had enough of it. Enough of him tormenting my family for no reason, enough of him having those pigs so close to our property, cannot eat in peace, just enough of everything. This time my dad said it is time to take things up in his own hands. Bear in mind, my dad and this man have been enemy for years, for no specific reason though. They are just a group of people you want to avoid.

The following Monday my dad was the first one in the parish councilor's office. These individuals deal with situations like this one, eager livestock too close to another individual. The health inspectors came, get a visual display of the situation and agrees that it is totally unacceptable. He heard about and came to start trouble, even with the health inspectors. He told them straight up that he was not going to change anything about the situation.

He was not going to relocate his animals, neither was he going to build a proper housing for them to limit the odor and squealing issue. It got so bad that to the point where the health inspectors threaten to tear down the current fencing for the pigs and just destroy everything. My mom tells them know just to give him a chance to do it on his own. The health inspectors gave him two weeks to get rid of it or else they were coming back to do it themselves. Two weeks passed; nothing changes. It was the hardest two weeks. Every single day Satan come to feed his pigs he cussed us. And all we did was ignore him.

We did not call the inspectors anymore as my dad hate to have to get officials involved in anything. The police, lawyers no one of that kind. I remember my mom talking to us all to bring the family some peace and oneness. She said, "you need to listen to me. Let us all go to God about this situation. This is bigger than us humans. This is Satan himself we are dealing with here. Let us fast and pray to God about him" and we all nod our heads in agreement. The last thing you want is a group of people that seek God for everything in their life before pursuing it to go to God in prayer for you because you are causing trouble. God mentioned in Luke 17:2 2 "It were better for him that a millstone was hanged about his neck, and he cast into the sea, than that he should offend one of these little ones". God was referring to those who have come to know him and possess the Christian qualities.

Believe me when I tell you, not even a month passed before he loses every single one of his pigs and their piglets. No, we did not physically murder his livestock, never doubt the power of praying. That was one of my very first proof of prayer. I know I always pray to God and things work but not as much as I prayed for God to do something about the problem of the pigs at the time. We did not pray what people would call "bad prayer" on his animals. We prayed that God may show up for us and defeat the enemy's plan. We prayed for strength to go on another day even after being accused wrongfully. We prayed for God to show him a sign that he was just a man, and that God is in control. We prayed for God to show him, who really is boss. And boy, did God show up! Oh yes, he did. Every week he lost one to two pigs.

Put the pieces together now. Couple weeks back we called the health inspectors on him. They threatened to destroy his livestock and then fast forward three weeks he is starting to lose his livestock? Strange right? No, that would be something I would say if I did not know how powerful prayer was. Of course, it was strange to him, so the accusations start again. "You all are witchcraft workers. You all poison my animals. You all throw evil powder in my pig pen" this man dragged my family through the community with these accusations. The good thing was everyone who he vents to defends us and dismantle his arguments.

My mom would be going about her business and got stopped by a random person in neighboring communities asking about what she did to pigs. Tell me now, Satan could not convince those in the communities with his lies, so he starts spreading rumors to different neighborhoods. But even then, people do not have to know you up close and personal to know what kind of person you are. As a result, his rumors were quickly put to rest. Another time god has been strong for us. It all came down to the truth which his brother told us that the pigs died from too much sun and hunger and a couple got hit by lighting. For whatever coincidence that happen everything was lined up to God's liking. He heard our cry and he said enough was enough.

This man has tried everything to get in our way. The river is the community's main source of water, a place for animal grazing, washing and just leisure time. As a result, it is almost impossible to not see your neighbors at the river. Because we believed in the idea that early bird catches the most worm, we would make our trips to the river early Saturday morning to fill up our drums using our donkey. It is not that we are going to ran out of water but it's most likely there are no one there and the water would be fresh and cleaner. Well, again I was wrong. Everywhere Satan presents himself, literally. As we start filling up our containers there, he went walking right above us. It was just as easy to walk behind us but no. When Satan has it out for you, only God can help you. Nothing you say or do will ever be able to change it. At this point all I wanted to do was run up to him and use one of the containers to knock him out then hold his head under the water and drown him. I was so angry I started crying. All I could hear was my mom's voice telling me that Satan just wants to get us in trouble. That was my constant reminder, every time I was faced with a situation involving him.

If walking above us while we are filling our containers was not enough, he would walk headfirst into our donkey going the opposite direction. It is a dirt track for Christ's sake, share the space. No, he is not going to move an inch to the right or left. He is walking as straight as an arrow. The worst part about this is not that the donkey is going to naturally get out of his way, but this man is always carrying a bucked by hand. So, one is on his head and the other in his hand. So just imagine taking up all that space plus extra, forcing you to go all the way to either side of the dirt track sometimes in tall shrubs depending on which part of the road you meet him. This mom was evil. I was starting to think he was possessed by some evil spirit. After all he was starting to lose his appearance becoming very ugly. He confessed to going to witchcraft workers to hurt us. Obviously, they did not do a decent job because nothing happened. We keep overcoming poverty, we keep becoming better humans in society.

With him losing his pigs, he was not giving up so easy. Are you thinking he was going to replace them? Oh yes, but not only did he replace them he add two cows and a goat. Now we do not only have to deal with pigs squealing but cows mooing and goat's maying. Just imagine those three sounds all at once ten feet away from your bedroom widows. The only escape we get are when we are not home or for a couple of hours at night when they are asleep. It was bizarre. Not only did we have to put up with more shit figuratively but literally. The rain would fall and let me tell you, our yard both front and back would be flooded with shit. Shit of all kinds. We could not look outside when it rains. We could not eat when it rains. We started getting sick. Every week someone else got sick. There is no point in talking to this evil man about nothing. Literally waste of time and energy. Not only did we have to put up with the noise and odor, but we now have shit to clean from animals that were not ours.

I kid you not when I say, this man finds any reason at all to start a fight with my family. This specific day he starts cussing us talking about how close our bathroom is to our kitchen. At the time everything was outdoors. Our shower, our toilet and our kitchen. At the back of my room was the kitchen and on the side was attached the shower in an enclosed zinc house. The location of this man livestock was sort of on a little hill. When you are up that high you can see right over our roof top. As a result, we always kept the windows facing his direction close. You do not need people like those knowing nothing about you.

What I do not understand is how someone that lives in a one-bedroom house with no kitchen and bathroom cuss someone with both attached to their house. This man even has chickens eager in his bedroom due to rain destroying a tiny portable coop he once had. Where did he get such high grounds to stand upon, making someone else's business his main concern? I find it mind blowing that one can be so invested in matters not concerning to him, feeling so powerful as if no one knows nothing about him. But people do, they just do not do him like he does people. Plus, he is enemy with more than three quarters of the community.

Even his own blood relatives would see us and apologize for him because of how he does us regularly. He has blood relatives that does not speak to him for years because of how toxic he is. He is the kind of person who hates to see another elevate. This man has given every neighbor a tough time. That, however, is not my story to tell.

This man tried to run me over with his car three years ago (2017) I had just returned from the exchange program for university students in the United States. I am quite sure he knew about that. He hates when you are elevating so much that he goes all out in making sure that you know, but this time he was about to go too far. I was standing across from his gate which is the main road on the right side and his house on the left. In Jamaica we drive on the left side. There was no specific reason I stopped at that spot. I would rather not be in eyesight distance of this evil man. I was just on my way to the

Sherrian Palmer-Barthol

community library with my sister-in-law when she mentioned something about my hair needing fixing. I remember pulling out my pocket mirror to see what was wrong.

This man was able to back out of his yard simply fine and just need to keep left to go about his business. But no, he chose to pull right over to my feet, on the right side of the road. He could have caused major accident for an oncoming vehicle. I did not even see the car because I was looking in the mirror. All I felt was my sister-in-law dragging my shirt and screaming "Sher" when I looked down, I see how close this man drove his car to me I start cussing. Just to tell you it was not a coincidence he kept looking in his mirror at me. I continued arguing and he pulled over on the side of the road and start arguing back at me.

This day I saw my parents bringing me cook meals on the other side of a cell. I saw his windshield and windows all shattered by the number of rocks I am going to throw at it. I saw my fist going through his face. I saw it all. But the last thing I saw was me walking across that stage to collect my degree and walking down the aisle to my gorgeous husband to be. I was not going to jeopardize my great future for a low life, uneducated bully and coward. With the help of my sister-in-law there that day I managed to calm down and recollect myself. It was one of the hardest days of my life because this man attacked me personally.

It is one thing to argue from a distance about my family, but this time it was personal. He mentioned in one of his rants that he will never stop until he sinks one of us, that day I feel as though he was out for me, and I was not going to let him off the hook that easy. I picked up my phone and called my dad immediately. No father wants to hear their little girl on the other side of the phone crying. That day I could not call my mom. I did not want to hear "leave it to god, let him fix it" because that's exactly what my mom would say. And even though I have proven God before and knows how much he was

87

able to do exceedingly abundantly above all I could ever ask or think, it felt like it was taking too long and I need some action right now, that very moment. Who else is better for some action than my dad? I remember my dad getting so upset he started stuttering and I could not hear a single word, so I hung up. When I get back from the library my mom told me that my dad went to his house, but he was not there. I was so hurt that day because I was attacked personally. I also called my fiancé, my now husband. He was so mad knowing there was nothing he could have done from where he is.

There is no specific place for this man to drag my family. He loves attention and a crowd. So, what better place to this on a Saturday when the river is packed by people sitting doing laundry. For me, this was the last string. It is one this to argue with us at our home, walk above us while catching water, does not share the road and concern about our living conditions. But to continue spreading lies and accusation about my family to a bunch of people who has no idea what is going was a whole different setting for me.

This time I confronted him personally, and we did kick it off. There was no backing down for me that day. We argued all the way to my home, and as usual he stopped by the animals, and we continued. This time around my mom did not stop me. She knew we all had enough.

Throughout the years of fighting and arguing with this evil man I call Satan one thing is always sure, no males were never around. Not that weekend though. For one reason or another, every single one of them was home. My brother that has always been close to him try to calm me down by telling me he will go and speak with him instead. Things did not go as planned. Satan starts disrespecting my brother bad and he was not having it. That specific brother is always the much calmer one. All my brothers are calm to say the least. The sisters are the ones with fire in their soul.

The next thing I know was that all four of my brothers was swinging machetes after this man. I still remember my mom holding Damian and begging him not to hurt Satan. My big sister Muno was holding Bobo and I think my nice grabbing his dad Garry, my eldest brother. That was the day I saw that man's life in a box six feet deep. I have no idea how the sound travels so far and fast but when I look, I saw two of my uncles with their machete running in the direction of the man. I have never had so much nerve and in a frenzy ever before in my life. I was not surprised at the way my brothers reacted. They know about everything that happened, they just never happened to be around.

I remember all of us sisters crying and begging them not to hurt him as he ran for safety in his parents' house. His own family were there as witnessed to everything but did nothing. Not one of them tries to defend him. How sad is that? His mom being a mom is going to automatically look out for his safety but that was the most that happen family wise. That was a day I will never forget, and neither will he. Because ever since that day he has put our family to rest finally. Or should I say my direct family. Eight long years this man, Satan has been putting me and my family through hell. Very shortly he started at my grandma then my uncle's wife, for reasons I do not care to know. All I know is, it sure feels good not being in hell and surviving what was meant to kill us.

What is your hell like situation? It may not have been anything close to mine or it may probably be worst. For whatever you consider it to be, take courage in God. Ask him for his guidance and direction. Lean not on your own understanding. The word of God says, "if anyone lacks knowledge ask of thee". As humans, we will always revert to the physical things of this world. Like defending ourselves in hell like situations but never forget that we are also complex spiritual beings. We have an advocate in Christ. It may feel as if it is taking too long waiting on him to work on your behalf, but he is always on time. Trust the process, trust his timing. If you recall the story of the three Hebrew boys thrown in the fiery furnace, God was there with them. Who knows? He was probably there preparing the way before them. The point is, God is standing during your battles, after all they belongs to him.

I could go on and on citing biblical examples of the goodness of God. But aren't we all familiar with those already? Yes, we are. I have so many individual experiences with God for myself. In January of 2010 I should have died. I should not have gotten out of that school bus alive. I should not have made it out of that chance, but God kept me. Everyone counts me out, but God said not yet. That school bus was completely written off but not my life. God was just preparing me to draft my story. Do not count yourself out because God is counting on you

Chapter Eight

MY JOURNEY TO FINDING TRUE LOVE

F inding love is a phase everyone experiences differently. For some it is through some sort of dating apps, some friends' suggestion, years of friendship that transpire into a love story or love at first sight. One is not to be judged about the way he or she wishes to pursue their intimate relationship. Love comes in all shape and form. From sending those good morning text messages and checking in to see if you ate to picking up your favorite bouquet of roses and watering your garden when you are away. Finding love comes easy, for others it comes after a lesson. My self personally can relate to the latter.

Of course, it would have been the one with the struggles for me. My entire life is built on a bundle of struggles and lessons learnt. Stemming from an extremely strict home, there were not really much room to have form a relationship. It was an environment where the term "boyfriend "was forbidden unless you want to pack your bag and head out. And by head out I mean leave and never return. My family was all I got and too important to me to risk that. And even though I was raised with three elder sisters, it was still not a safe space to express your feelings on that topic. For my parents, the term boyfriend only rings one bell for them, "pregnancy ". They told the story a million time of how they start having kids at an early age and how it in some ways hinder them from becoming educated and that they will not sit idle and watch the same thing happen to us.

I grew up all my teenager life scared of boys. I do not want to be seen close to them, holding hands, hands over shoulder nothing because to me I would have been dead. I dread been seen walking home from school with a friend. The only boys I was somewhat comfortable talking to are the ones I meet when I go to different church branches. With these boys I do not normally get such a dread stare from my parents and siblings, and you could figure why. Growing up in the church and not just any church. (The apostolic church) the stakes are high, and the rules and code of conduct are the whole nine yards.

The rules of the church state that you can only be married to a member of a church and of the same apostolic faith. So of course, when my family sees me getting close to a church brother they do not stare so much. After understanding that church rule, it never sits well with me. I questioned it all the time and I would always get schooled with the Bible verse that speaks about unequally yoked. Of course, the verse specifically said 'with unbelievers' but for some reason they always overlooked that part because it does not support their agenda.

You come under a lot of pressure being a teenager and not able to talk to your parents or family members about boys. You are being judged by the church and everyone else around you except one group of people, your friends. My friends were the only ones I could talk to about boys and know that I was not going to be judged. And the sad part is, a lot of times these teenage friends does not have the right answers for you and if you are lightheaded, later in life you will have a lot of regrets all from being young and dumb.

What I was never able to grasp was the way in which apostolic young adults go about finding a husband. Remember now, boyfriends are a sin in the apostolic doctrine, for the most part in the church I was brought up in. Husband is the ideal. But do you not need a boyfriend first to be your husband? Well, not exactly in their rule book. I had two sisters who have found their current relationship in the church, so I have a little knowledgeable how they went about it. So, for starters, if you see someone you like within your church branch, either party then make a move to let the other one knows their interest. If each party agrees in the interest the next move is to notify the leaders of both churches about it.

This is important if you do not want to be ridiculed and embarrassed by the leaders of your church if the news of you two having any form of love affair reaches their ears before you tell them. After this is done there is then a meeting with both parties, their parents and their pastors. This meeting usually set the boundaries of things they can and cannot do within the time of getting to know each other. This phase they refer to it as courting. No kissing, no touching, among others.

First, they lost me when I must get my pastors involved. We are not some kind of animals that operates strictly off mating. We have emotions. We feel loved, we show love. Going through all that only confined what was meant to be shared with each other. Okay, I understand that their focus is putting in as many boundaries to prevent sex before marriage. I get it, but why not just said that. Oh no, they cannot because even the word 'sex' was never mentioned once in my years of going to that church.

Do not even think you will just wake up one day and be surprised at this charming hotel or restaurant with a spontaneous engagement. That is not how it is done in the church. The groom as to visit the bride to be church with his pastor, friends and families if he chose and the engagement is done right before the entire congregation. That right there, was probably the last string for me. What about our special moment? It was all a shit show to me, and I could not afford to put myself through that.

If you check the rate of young adult who has walk away from the Apostolic church, it is alarming. Young adults have a challenging time growing in this specific church branch. Not only that, but you also come under a lot of pressure even before you reach twenty-five because what happened is that, sometimes all the men are already married and the ones that are not does fit in your requirements. Not only are you judged for not being in a relationship by that time, but you are also told how fussy you are, and you want this perfect guy when God has one right in front of you. Excuse me? Are you God! How is it that my ambition is now turned into stubbornness and selfishness? It was as though they want to pick this guy for you, and you should just take him and move on. First, I lived in a free country with the will to do whatever I want.

In my late teenage years, I started getting close with a fellow church brother. He was a friend of my sister's husband. We got introduced over the phone briefly after my sister's engagement. At the time, it started out as me being his spiritual mentor. I was very strongly embedded in the faith. As time goes by, he starts attending family dinners and outings and quickly became good friends with my family. It was a bit uncomfortable for me at first. I love to have my different relationship separate from my family life if you know what I mean. Friends at school stay at school, church friends stay at church. It was becoming more coming. He was showing up at my house everything my now brother-in-law would come by. The youth from my church quickly starts speculating and refer to us as a couple.

First, I had no emotional connection with this young man. No physical appeal, nothing at all. I saw this guy as nothing but a friend but overtime he starts becoming extremely comfortable. Sending me good morning messages. Always want to know what is going on and right before I go to bed. I quickly realize a pattern. But being cooped up all my life I had no idea how to deal with this. Do I go tell my mom? Do I tell my sisters? Who exactly do I talk to? Second, I was eighteen years old and still going to school, getting ready for college, still living under my parents' roof so that was a red flag. As such I kept my mouth shut. A couple of mornings after he start addressing me as 'beautiful', 'sweetie' and so in. My naive self just think it was a courteous thing and he was just being nice. All I kept doing was laughing. Pretty dumb right? I know.

Time would not spare me to share all the excellent details that transpire but what I will say is I have wasted a year of my life being stupid, acting irresponsible and dumb. That was my very first actual relationship which ends in a sour turn all because of not knowing. There is simply nothing wrong with educating your children on this matter, it will probably save them a world of hurt and regrets. Friends can never know what a parent knows because they are just a struggling dumb soul as your kid. Parents have knowledge and experience they can impart.

I started university as a wounded soul. I was hurt by those I thought would comfort and protect me. As a result, my passion and drive for the church was falling day by day. I would still read my Bible and pray but that enthusiasm was gone. I have always dress modestly and wear nonrevealing clothing, but the extent to which I usually go I stopped. I get okay with wearing a skirt that would be considered a little too short for me and so on. Being away from families and the church give me that space to truly find myself. That space where I was always walking in chalk line.

Unbelievably, I have spent the first twenty years of my life being brainwashed with rules and guidelines. I do certain things because if I do otherwise, I was going to be called out by the church, or I acted a certain way because my mom think it is godlier. For twenty years I was tossed by the wind doing what everybody else wants me to do, I was just about over it.

In the year 2015 I started a relationship with a guy that I knew had a crush on me since high school. What are the odds that he was also a Christian? Well, they were high. I have always liked his personality and his charming spirit. What I remembered before getting into a relationship with him was that he was in a relationship in high school with a girl who was then going to the same university as myself. H told me they were over and of course I believed him. We started hanging out like once every two months for about Seven months. I think this time we have created a great emotional and physical connection. He was handsome to say the least. We kind of click. We get each other. This one my mom knows about, but once more he was only a good friend of mind that is also a Christian. I could not use the term boyfriend.

I Could not help but think though that my mom knew more than I thought. Every time I would call her, and she would ask me how my little friend is. My mom even starts giving him food provisions to take to me whenever he was coming to Kingston. Of course, I told my mom that he was just coming to see his girlfriend which goes to the same school as me. Such a lie. I was the girlfriend. I am quite sure my mom did not believe a word I said. My mom always speaks highly of him as a respectable and humble young man, but even then, he was not without flaws.

The fact that you called yourself a Christian and your dad is a pastor does not give you the pass of being a fornicator. I had just turn twenty-one years old and was stoked about it. Legal to do a lot of things. Own a home, drive a car etc. At this age I was just trying to find back myself. Find who I really am exactly. But for him, he wanted more. More than what I could give at the time. I was falling so hard for him I almost lose sight of what was before me. Simply put, he wanted sex. Yes. Primarily, I have no idea how to have sex, and secondly, I was not about lose my family for having sex before marriage. I remember asking for some time to think this through and he said yes.

Only to find out within my time of thinking he was busy with some other female. I can remember feeling distant from him emotionally. It was as if I am now searching for something I did not have. I was confused and could not seem to stop panicking.

Is this how this relationship thing work? I thought to myself. One party gets busy with someone else because they are not disciplined enough to wait. I was confused. I thought he was different you know. Raised in the church just like myself so I figured I would have a better shot with him. Not so much. What I did realize that though, was that the standards for females within the church are held ten times higher than those of the males. A male can impregnate a female and still comes to church to lead praise and worship (not in my church though) while the females must stay home and hide from all the stigma and shame from getting pregnant out of wedlock.

As time goes by, I realized that someone else was now in the picture. I was hurting so bad. This was my very first live story and one of the strongest emotional connections I have experienced in my life. So, letting go was hard. But holding on I was just hurting myself more. That was when I experienced my first heartbreak. The one that have you not eat, not sleep just crying all the time. I left hundreds of phone calls and text messages on his phone with no reply until I was forced to give up. Day by day I start getting better. Getting dressed up and acting all cute once more. I was still hurting though. This lasted until late summer of 2016, and I finally let go. Well, I did not. I was forced to let go once more.

The fact that nobody told me the dangers of jumping into a relationship while hurting from a past romance, still to this day make me hate this whole section of this love affair, I am going to share with you. And even though it did not last for more than six months it is still to this date where ninety nine percent of my regrets in life came from.

All my life I have always have big dreams and great ambitions. I knew the type of men that I am attracted to and what I was willing to settle far. For the most part. This specific summer I was not so sure. The same summer that I was starting to get over my heart rake I met someone. Someone that does not have a job, no education, no assets nothing and was not a Christian. This person survives by burning movies unto digital virtual disk and then walks around into neighboring communities and sell them for one hundred dollars each. Equivalent of less than one US dollars. So do the math.

I was home for the last part of summer, healing from my breakup and spending time with my family when this guy showed up at our gate. One of my big sisters were there and ask me to go get a couple of movies for her. I went but did not came back as fast as I should as he tried to have a conversation with me. First off, I have never seen this young man in my life. My family members have but I have never. After all I was only home for the summer break.

He started a conversation asking about me. What is my name, where I am from and of course my phone number? I have always been polite and have a big problem with stopping people in their tracks sometimes. He asked for my number, and I remember giving it to him. I do not normally give out my number like that. Heartbreak makes you do crazy stupid stuff. I remember walking away telling him that the fact that I gave him my number does not mean I am going to reply to him. And he said OKAY he understands.

About two weeks passed and he has not message me, and I totally forgot about him because I was still set on getting my boyfriend back. Even after one hundred and fifty unanswered messages. I was still trying. He gets tired of me and finally blocked my number and on all social media platform.

What are the odds that about two days after this, the DVD guy that I gave my number text me? Well, he did. Feeling hurt and heartbroken at the time felt like this new attention I was getting was the best thing in the world. In a matter of weeks, I went from crying eyes to big smiley face. I was feeling myself once more. Or that was what I thought. This young man starts showing up more than usual in my area. Of course, I cannot be seen with him, and he cannot come to my house. So as a result, I would always hide away to my uncle's house that is also my neighbor since they were all good friends. I would spend an hour or so by then just for a chance to talk to him. Before soon my mom caught up on us. I must deny there was nothing going on. Not because I was so scared of my mom anymore, but because of I was ashamed of him.

He was not one of the better-looking young men I have seen. Simply put he was ugly, his mouth was bugged, he was very black, uneducated, jobless, just the whole nine yards. He was not on my list. Even though I realized that very soon, I still loved having him in my corner. And before you all judged me, I am not a user. I had him in my corner because without him all I feel was hurt, anger and pain. It was about four months now into our secret relationship and he wants to make it public. After all, who wants to be hiding such a beautiful, intelligent girl as me. For him, he thinks the best way to make it public was by getting my mother's blessing.

Just so you know, my mother has shared her displeasure about him, and for once I support my mom's decision regarding my love life. He was not for me. I deserved way better. As a result, I encourage him to go speak with my mother because I had already told my mom about him and that she should turn him down. At this point I was just over this fruitless, barren relationship. It was not for me. While he was planning on all the cute things he was going to say to my mother, I was rejoicing in the inside to know I will be getting rid of him finally. If only I knew what was ahead.

He finally went to my mom one night she was getting ready for church. My mom did not have the time to have the talk with him, so she just made it plain and simple. She told him she knew what he was there for, and it is a no because I deserved better and then told him to have a good night. Oh my god! That was one of my mom's coldest moments, but I was not sorry she did it.

The next day I get the news from both him and my mom. He did not take the news very well and thought my mom was rude. I stopped him in his track and told him it is whatever my mom says. That did not sit right with him. He then goes in to ask if I was going to choose my mom over him. Say what now? That was my last thread. Of course, the answer is a million times over. This is my mother we are talking about here. Who exactly do he think he is? We had a huge explicit argument and then proceed to block him on my social media pages. Before I could even finish, he was already dragging both my mom and I on Facebook.

He was not dealing with the breakup at all. At least this time, I was on the other end of the breakup stick. I was making the shots and doing what was best for me. This guy uses to visit me occasionally while I was living in Kingston for school, so he knows where I lived. I did not have a single taught of changing my address for what is there to worry about right? Well, I should have been worried. In the middle of the night, banging on grills demanding me or anyone who was disturbed by the cracking of steels, to let him in. There was this one door on our building that is rarely ever locked, and he made use of it. This young man has soon turned into a demon possess psychotic being.

He would show up everywhere I was. Asked me how he knew, I have no idea. He wants an explanation as to why we cannot be together and oh how I gave it to him. I told him he was uneducated and unintelligent, entitled, how much his teeth gave me anxiety and his sweaty odor was disturbing. Lastly, I told him he was ugly. I am usually a very polite person, but this young man requires too much. As if being clingy and wanting to come by my boarding accommodation every other week was not enough for him, he would call after every time after a five-minute delay message gap.

This guy feared me breaking up with him to the point where he was crazy and controlling the entire time, we were together. He bragged about how much he is dating the most beautiful girl on the planet. That he was right about. But I knew from the get-go that I could not be with him. Pain makes you do stupid things. Breaking up with him was easy, the hard part was the aftermath. He took to social media the issue and oh how much he had to say. I had blocked him so mind you I was not able to see what he was posting but my best friend could. She would send me the screenshots of what he was saying and told me it was getting bad I need to address it. This happened a week before I came to the United States for the first time in the J1Student exchange program in May of 2017.

I knew in my head that there was no way I was going to come back to Jamaica and still be dealing with this issue. I remember reaching out to his aunt and making a complaint about his behavior on social media. Before I could even leave the Island, the issues were put to rest for the most part. He would still throw his shades and so on, but I would never give him a reaction because that is all he wants to take it as encouragement to continue insulting. Frank, I understand his frustration. Losing a girl like me is going to break your heart, because I come with the full package.

So yes, that chapter of my life is one I don't talk about, I hate myself for putting myself in that position in the first place, and I regret every second of that relationship and hated every bone that compose his beings. I hated him, still hates him and will forever hate him. I was so focused on hurting the guy that I once loved that I dive headfirst into a relationship with a guy I did not even know, only to end up hurting myself. Yes, that was very stupid of me, but it is all in the learning processes. I put my life in this book for all you to read about my stories. Take whatever you can from my experiences and learn from my mistakes. As that chapter of my love life came to an abrupt ending, I could not even begin to imagine what the good lord had in store for me.

The Lord works in mysterious ways. I can attest to that. May 2017 I was all ready for the J1 Exchange program. But before I further comment on that let me take you a little way back. In November of 2015 I started an application or that same above-mentioned program. I did my paperwork and my passport, and everything was looking good except one problem. I could not come up with half of the program fee by the end of December that said year. And by the next February I would need the full payment to make it on the programmatic of 2016. I started talking to my family members about it, but we were very tight on the financial end.

That said year my biggest sister Kay, told me that if things work out all right for her when she traveled to the United States for the first time, she will make sure to send me on the program. As such I cancelled that year while looking forward to starting the process once again in November of 2017. My sister went abroad, and she delivered as promised. She paid all my fees for me. From the application down to my flight. I was excited. In the middle of the process, I got my job placement replaced three times. I was so agitated with my agency.

At first, I was supposed to go to South Dakota, then it got changed to North Carolina and then finally to Missouri. Not only was I upset at the idea that placements keep getting arranged, but I was also mad because my final placement did not sound fun to me. I have never heard of the State Missouri before the program. I further went on google earth to get a better view of the location where I would be living and staying for the time. I was a bit surprised in some areas. Branson specifically was a tourist hotspot. There were a lot of things to do and a lot of opportunities for second job. Jamaicans pride themselves on getting a second job sometimes even third. We find every way to make extra-legal money. We have people to repay for helping us on the program and in most cases tuition fees. After getting off my laptop, I thought to myself, it is not that bad after all.

May seventeen kay took me to the Norman Manley International Airport in Kingston. I still remember that outfit. A blue spaghetti strap dress with a zipper running diagonally in the front with a red open front cardigan. It was my first time in an airport and taking a flight. I was scared and nervous but mostly overly excited that I was willing to do it all because of my sister.

That said year, she sacrificed the purchasing of a plot of land just to be able to help me on the program. It was a big sacrifice. One that I will never forget. And one that a lot of family members would not make. Every opportunity I get I always tell her how grateful I am to her for risking it all just to help a non-deserving sister as me. Non deserving in the sense that she owed me nothing, I have no special talent or features, she could have easily gone ahead an buy her plot of land. I still do not know why she did it, but looking back, I would have done the same thing for any siblings needing help.

I took roughly 3 hours to get to my destination. I was picked up by my new employer. His vibrant spirit immediately cheered me up and I quickly become comfortable. I was one of the first student to make it to his company that year. As a result, I was given the option of choosing which rooms I wanted to be in. It was all a blank slate since you do not really know who your roommates going to be. I trusted my gut and I did not regret my decision. My roommate was the sweetest soul and was like a little sister to me the entire time. We formed a friendship of which we still maintain to date.

It was now our first day of work. everyone was stoked. We were going to meet new people and have a new normal for four long summer months. I cannot remember truly clear what my first day of work was like. I remember the bus ride to work and being introduced to the head housekeepers and receptionist but that is it for the most part. What I cannot forgot was that day I met my now husband and every day after that.

It was in Room 324 in the main building. Working as a housekeeper, it was my job to clean the guest bedrooms and provide amenities. I was already making bed for two weeks, so I pretty much got the hang of it. This specific morning, I was minding my business as always and singing while stripping the bed. About five minutes in, I saw this young man walked into the room I was cleaning. He explained to me that he was the one assigned to strip the beds and so forth. I told him I got it covered for that room, but he could go ahead and take care of my other rooms on the list. As he was about to walk out, he said, "by the way I am Billy" as he reached out his arms to me and I walked forward putting my hand in his palm saying "I'm Sherry nice to meet you" after that handshake, I do not know what happened.

I remember running to my roommate and telling her about meeting Billy. I felt butterflies telling her the story. To my surprise she had already met him. Turns out Billy worked in the breakfast area some days before. For me, that morning was the first I have seen this young man. It led me to think that destiny had it to be like that. We both shared a special moment, and it was more obvious with him because his face turned red. A minute after, he came to the room that I ran into. He said, "by the way, you have a beautiful voice" oh my god. Did he just complement me? I did not know how to act.

For a moment there, I saw my future flashed before my eyes. I saw us together, traveling the world, owning big companies and having the cutest babies ever. I have seen it all. I felt butterflies that entire day and every day after that that we see each other. It did not take long for us to start having little conversations here and there. Before you know it, he was bringing me coffee and donuts every now and then. I was really enjoying his company. I could not help but noticed that for about three consecutive days he has not showed up to work. We did not exchange number or social media accounts. I missed him a lot and wants to know what was going on.

On the third day I asked one of the head housekeepers for his phone number, but she did not have it. I then asked this little boy, who was the grandson of my employer since he was remarkably close to Billy. Sadly, he did not have it as well. I was heartbroken. What I did not know was that his mom was the receptionist and his stepdad the maintenance guy. But we will talk about that further on. Thursday morning comes I was sad and did not have the urge to go to work, but I really do not have any choice. I had no hopes of seeing him, since people leave their jobs all the time. I was in the laundry room stacking my cart and getting ready to start my day cleaning.

I suddenly hear footsteps. Yes, it is normal, but these sounds familiar. More manly if I should say. And there he was. He walked in and was like, "Hey, I heard you were asking for me and asked for my number". I said, "yes, I was. I did not see you for a couple of days and was a bit worried about you". He then wrote his number on the back of one of the hotel's card and hand it to me. I still have it to date. I said thank you and he walked off. Two seconds later he was back, and we were kissing.

Well, I did not see it coming. But what I do know is that our first kiss was spectacular and one I will never forget. I quickly add his number to my contact, and we never stop talking. Like literally. I could not keep this good news to myself so once again I ran to my roommate and told her I just got Billy's number and a kiss. She was so happy and was just screaming in excitement. This was in the third week of June. The week after I invited him over to the apartment I was staying in at the time. He spent a couple of days and, on the Friday, June 30th, 2017, we had our first date. We walked to this creek side park. It has a gazebo, a tennis court and a basketball court. It was pretty and it was my idea. I remember sitting under that gazebo, we both share some very deep and personal part of our life. We had a connection. We have been texting for over a week and all but sharing these personal details of our life face to face was extremely passionate. That was the first time he told me he loved me. And without hesitation I said it back. There was no need for contemplation.

I knew what we share was special. We then went for a walk to the creek. He would not let me walk through the rubbles. He feared me falling, so he picks me up and carried me the entire way. We had so much fun. We talked about him wanting to join the military, me finishing my bachelor's degree and just future aspirations. I had the pleasure of catching a couple of crawdads. Fun story, after overturning the first stone, I screamed, "I saw a shrimp". The look on Billy's face was like, what? I repeated myself because I thought he did not hear or understood what I said. Only to find out that shrimps does not live-in creek. You could have fooled me. All my life I have grown up calling anything with claws and live in the river shrimp. We laughed so hard. We came home and enjoy our night learning more about each other.

To date, I am still grateful for the time we took then just learning more about each other and not like the typical relationship that normally started with the physical aspects. My employer quickly finds out about our rapidly growing relationship, of course this is America. People just cannot seem to mind their own business. I did not know how he was going to react being that we are both employees at his company. Turns out I was worried for nothing. He was so supportive of us and would make sure we both have the same days off so we could spend more time together.

Life at work start becoming more better. I get to see the guy I love almost every day. The surprises, the treats, random kissing in the elevators, stairways, kitchen just about anywhere. I could not contain myself. I would just blush all day. With all this comes one big problem. I start falling back on the number of rooms I get done in a certain time. But a girl can do. I was faller super-fast and hard in love with this guy. I would be cleaning my room and see him through the window outside and would just stay their stare and melt. I would blush so hard. This love affair was growing extremely fast, and I could not go in any further without telling my parents about it. Mind you, I have never told my parents about a boy, and secondly, I was scared.

What if they do not want me to be with someone out of my culture or race? I mean they never spoke about those things so I would not know. It was just a ton of what ifs. My parents were so accepting and supportive. I then told my siblings and my best friends. Having this kind of support system make life so much easier. Surround yourself with people you know are going to be genuinely happy and supportive for you. I then start to invite him over to my apartment more often as a means of spending time together. We would go on walks together while still getting to know each other. I remember the first night he made me dinner.

Mind you I have never had a guy made me dinner. It was not your ordinary chicken and rice. It was well marbled rib eye stake with sautéed mushroom and onions in a sweet glaze. He also made a salad with romaine lettuce and mushroom with bell peppers. To be honest with you, everything looks and smell amazing until it was time to eat. He served the steaks sliced in little strips making it easier to eat which was nice of him. But I could not help but notice that majority of the inner steak was 'uncooked'. We are talking about a Jamaican girl here who is used to meat cooking through and through, and when it is not, we say it is either raw or undercooked. This young man puts a lot of effort into the meal. Being the person I am, I can be very forward at times. But this is not just anybody this is the person

107

I was falling fast and hard for. Should I tell him it is undercooked? I keep asking myself.

I sat and looked at the food for a solid minute before trying it. It did not take long before he notices that I was not eating. He asked if I was ok and if everything was all right. I smiled and said yes, followed by but. He said, "but what baby girl" that is the name he has called me from the first date. My heart was pounding currently. Am I going to break his heart? Is he going to think that I am being ungrateful to him for his effort and time? All these thoughts going through my head, but I could not resist. As such I answered him saying, "babe, I am not sure, but I think the meat is a little undercooked because blood is coming out of it" I held my head down in shame. I just broke his heart. Well, not so fast. It was in that moment he taught me that the red substance was not blood, but rather hemoglobin. He asked me to just try it and if I did not like it then I would not have to eat it neither feeling bad because I did not. I grabbed my fork and gather some of the sauteed mushrooms and onions with a piece of steak and boy was I wrong. It was the most tender piece of meat I have had in my life. The line of fat that just explodes in my moth releasing a ton of flavor is just indescribable.

I looked into his eyes and saw his world lit up with my reaction. It was a priceless moment. One to this date we still share with our families and friends. It was in that moment he has received the confirmation, that his arduous work and effort were appreciated and was very well worth every second. His steaks are still my favorite and I just can't bring myself to eat a steak meal if it is not prepared by my husband. He now has an updated version of his spices and herbs which bring out a ton more of other flavor in the meat. And what can I say? I am here for it all. I could tell you a lot more of my favorite dish that he makes but that would take away the time for more advanced aspect in our relationship.

Engagements are important. Every little girl dream of the wedding day in a princess dress. Even if they change their mind when they grow up. We imagine the entire scenario of our prince charming popping the question. To be honest, I never really have a specific idea of what I want my engagement to be, but I knew that whenever I find the one that my heart is yearning for, the answer will be yes. I did not see a thousand roses or a chariot with white horses. I saw a man who was selfless, respects me, respects my family, prioritize family time and is extremely ambitious. I saw a man who puts Jesus at the center of his life and loves me for who I am. Yes, I saw a man on one knee in my apartment bedroom while I was undressing out of my work uniform.

Let me take you back a little bit. When I came on the student exchange program, I was just coming out of a broken relationship as I mentioned before. One that I should not have been in from the beginning. As a result, I told myself that I was going to give this dating life up until I was able to find myself again. Therefore, I bought myself a ring from the dollar tree. I told myself that I am going to wear this ring to not have boys approaching me, and if they do, I will tell them I am married. For some reason I was not wearing the ring the morning I met Billy, my now husband. After things get serious with us, I started wearing the ring once more. One day out of nowhere, he asked me what the size of the ring I am wearing. I quickly replied size eight. Afterall, what was the arm in that.

To me at the time, it was just a question. Not taking into consideration that this the young man who disciplined a coworker because he was talking sexually to me. The same young man who would not let me walk through the rubbles because he feared me getting hurt. This young man has love me unconditionally through it all. This was the young man I had just gave my ring finger size to without thinking. And I am so glad I did. He bought the cutest champaign gold diamond ring for me. It was just small and unique and just my type.

There in the bedroom, on his knees he asked me to marry him with the sweetest romantic music playing in the background. What am I supposed to do now? I have never been proposed to before. When I saw him on one knee, I started crying and fell to the floor. All I remember saying was no! no! no! This guy that I was madly in love with asked me to spend the rest of my life with him and I said no. am I crazy? No, I am not. I was not saying no to the engagement. I just could not believe that it was happening.

I should have seen it coming. I have gotten all the signals. That said night before the engagement, he showed up at my second job, a restaurant. I was incredibly surprised to see him. He told me that he was just checking in on me and want to have lunch with me on my lunch time. I did not get off work until ten PM that night. I asked him to just stay and wait for me since he was going to sleep at my place that night, but he insisted he must go do something first then he will have to come back to get me. I thought to myself, okay no big deal. He asked for my apartment keys, kissed me and left. No big deal right. Turns out he went to my apartment, decorate my bedroom in rose petals and make dinner. All my housemates knew about it except me. I was blindfolded into the apartment.

After I took a minute to recollect myself, I told him the biggest yes and he slid that diamond on my finger. We enjoyed a great dinner and have the most comfortable sleep that night. Waking up knowing that I get to have a thousand more days like that waking up to him gives me butterfly to date.

Unbelievably, answering the proposal question was not half as hard as me telling my parents. I am from a culture where the groom always gets the parents blessing before an engagement. In our case, Billy did not. At the time he did not understand a word in Jamaican creole and that was all my dad speaks. Of course, he could not have let me speak on behalf of him because that would have ruined the surprise. Just how do I tell my parents that I am now engaged to this guy that I had only known for two months, and I was just finishing college. Days pass before I mentioned a word about it. I was a wreck. I remember calling my mom telling her that Billy gave me a 'promise ring'. I explained to her that the meaning behind the ring was that no matter where we go over this world, we will always find each other back. Wow, what a way to put 'I am going to spend the rest of my life with this guy'. My mom tries to understand from my standpoint, and I could not appreciate it anymore.

Of course, she wants Billy to come to Jamaica and ask for their permission for my hand in marriage. They want it to be done the right way from start to finish. The idea of bringing home my then fiancé sounds good, and I would not want anything more than to do just that except one big problem. Our hosting conditions. At the time we did not have the amenities that would make him most comfortable like an indoor kitchen and bathroom. That for us was important.

My parents have been so supportive of me from the very first moment I told them about Billy. And even though he did not get the chance to visit Jamaica before our wedding, my parents welcomed him into our family with wide open arms. That summer of 2017 after sharing our engagement with family and friends, we spend every waking moment together. After all we only had two months left before I had to go back to Jamaica, and he would be going to Georgia at Fort Benning for Basic training for the Army. We visit amusement parks, the lake, the malls and live shows. We were more comfortable being together.

I always heard him speak of the Military and how much he wants to join it. I would ask him about it all the time until one day he finally decided to take the step. Mind you I was very skeptic of military member. Just this stigma surrounding them about how arrogant and abusive they were, and I was not about that life. His grandmother picked us up that day and we went to the recruiter's office located in downtown Branson, Missouri.

It was an immensely proud moment, and I am grateful I was able to share in that moment with him. For the next couple of weeks, he was terribly busy dealing with Military stuff and it was hard not having him around that often, but he did what he had to, and I had was to understand. The following week he spent every day with me at one of the company's hotel my employer placed me since they were cleaning the apartment and it was almost time to go back to Jamaica.

Initially, we both have our flights for the same day, September 12, 2017. However, they both got canceled because of the weather conditions. As such, I flew to Jamaica on the 13th, and he flew to Georgia on the 14th. Our hearts were broken. We both dread what was ahead of us. The what if's, the uncertainty, complete panic, it was a nightmare. We did not have anything to held on to other than the memories that we have created. Or did we have something better? Yes, we did. We had trust. And hand in hand with all the memories we had, we combined them together with a lot a love and that was what we cling to.

One of the first thing I told my husband then was that I would never be with a military guy. I have seen scenarios way too often in my culture where military personnel have this manufactured anger in their personal life and always ending up taking their life and their partners life as well. It was scary for me, but I was falling hard for him. One day he sat me down and explain to me how the military works here in the United States. I became a little more acceptance of it. After all I was not going to stand in between him and his dream.

How are we going to do this long-distance relationship? How am I going to go four months without talking to him every day? It was just a myriad of questions circulating in my head. I was freaking out a lot. I heard a lot of myths and stories about being in a military relationship. But having firsthand experience of it makes all the difference. Billy spent four months, from September 2017 to January 2018 in Basic training Fort Benning, Georgia. Every single day after going back to Jamaica I would write a letter to him. I would send a weeks' worth in one batch in the weekend.

Getting his address from his commander takes roughly a month after he was already there. Anxiety and worry set in. What if he is hurt? Is he adjusting, ok? Is he being bullied? Does he still love me? Yes, I know it sounds weird, but I could not help but ask myself that question. There is this old saying that goes, "Out of sight, out of mind" and I was starting to believe it until I remember our promise that we would use trust to pull through. Around a month and a half after him being in Georgia he got a phone call pass. My phone rang three thirty-two in the morning and I woke up immediately. I had a new ringtone set for him that way I never missed his call since we were in different time zone. His voice made my entire month. I could not stop crying while we were there talking on the phone. He did not have much time, but he makes sure to call me first to remind me that he still loves me, how much he misses me and that seals it for me. I get off the phone with the brightest smile and with so much more confidence that I still have my true love out and we were going to pull through.

The process of sending mail is already hectic as it is coming from an international source into the United States. But going to be disburse it at a military facility is far more challenging. The amount of sorting and processing required before it gets to the designated person is astounding. My letters never get to Billy until after three weeks, sometimes a month.

Before the phone call we were both worried sick because of no communication. He was not getting my mail soon enough and I was not getting any from him because I had forgotten to give him my Jamaican address before he went to Georgia. Now he must wait until he had received one of my letters to get the senders' address. It was a painful time for both of us but that one phone call brings about so much hope and reassurance that we still have each other. As time goes by, he would have gotten more phone call passes and was able to send me letters. My letters were still taking too long so I decided to use this app called Sandbox to send my letters. It cost three US dollars per letter, but it was worth it since we could attach a couple of photos to the letter as well and it only takes three days for it to be delivered.

Communication begins to flow more smoothly, and it was amazing. We both had a lot of lonely nights. Crying ourselves to sleep nights. Nights we had huge arguments because of miscommunication. But no matter what it was we always pull through together. It was never me against my husband, or my husband against me, but both of us against the problem or situation at hand.

It was now approaching his graduation date. I knew the first thing I want to take care of after returning from the exchange program was my United States visitor's Visa. So, on October second, 2017, I went for my Visa interview at the United States embassy. It was surprisingly an exceptionally smooth process. No ambush, no interrogation. I was just asked what my reason was to visit and what was my current Grade Point Average at the time. I was granted a ten-year visitor's visa. One of the best days of my life. I would not know what to do with myself if I was not able to celebrate in that special moment of him graduating.

On December twenty eight I flew to the United States to spend time with his family since we would be driving from Missouri to Georgia on January the 10th 2018. For love nor money I have not traveled on the 10th of January since January 10th, 2011. That was the date of a major accident I was a part of in the 10th grade. His graduation was January 12th, 2018. It was a twelve-hour drive but for some reason I was not fearful in the least. I was just looking forward to kissing my fiancé at the time. We made it safe to Georgia and was able to spend the turning blue ceremony, graduation day and a couple of days after with him. It was a great feeling. I flew back to Jamaica on January fifteenth the same day he had to return to the military base. It was short but it was fun while it lasted.

Now that he was now a graduate and was moving on to his first duty station, he gets to have his phone all the time now. It was the best thing ever. We talked every day. We were able to smooth and bring clarity to a couple of things a lot better. It was in April of 2018 when we announced we were going to get married June 30th, 2018. I was happy to have my family's blessing and encouragement through it all. In May of 2018 I headed off to the United States once more on the exchange program. Only this time I was not by myself. My elder sister Roxann was there with me on the same program, working at the same place. It was a pleasure having her join me.

Secondly, I was not just coming to work, I was coming to get married to my fiancé, my favorite human being who was based and serving in Joint Base Elmendorf-Richardson, Alaska. (JBER). My sister and I was working in his hometown Branson, Missouri, the same town where we met. My best friend as well would be joining us from Florida and my big sister Kay would also be joining us from Jamaica. I was overwhelmed with love, peace and oneness but I could not help but feel out of place. Something was missing. My parents. Yes, my parents were not able to join us, and I could not feel more out of place.

They were supposed to be there. My dad should be walking me down the aisle while my mom sits in the front row with the biggest smile on her face knowing I have made her proud once more. But all that did not happen. It was beyond all of us control. My dad was in the middle of getting his birth certificate replaced and my mom was not going to leave my dad alone there.

Our wedding was small, intimate and surrounded by the ones we love and loves us in the same measure. But it was not complete without my parents and that is why my husband, and I will be renewing our vow our earliest possible chance we get to go to Jamaica. We owed that to my parents to say the least. If the situation was reversed, I am quite sure my husband's side of the family would not have taken it the way my parents did and for that I have appreciate them even more and want to do it the right way. We got married on June 30th, one of the best days of my life. We had a great six-day honeymoon before my husband had to head back to Alaska.

Once again it was great while it lasted. You might by now noticed a pattern. We are always leaving. We rarely get to spend much time with each other. But the beauty in those time is that it gives you something to look forward to. The never-ending anticipation. It keeps things fresh and exciting. But the struggle comes in when you just need that long hug after a long grueling day. You just want to sit on the couch and have coffee and just relax.

Those are the hard parts which no one wants to talk about. Finding love for me comes in waves. It was not easy. I have had my share of sleepless night. But the light at the end of the tunnel was worth the struggles of the journey. 1 Corinthians 13:4-8, "Charity suffered long, and is kind; charity envieth not; charity vaunteth not itself, is not puffed up, doth not behave itself unseemly, seeketh not her own, is not easily provoked, thinketh no evil; Rejoiceth not in iniquity, but rejoiceth in the truth; bearers all things believe all things, hopeth all things, endureth all things. Charity never faileth: but whether there be prophecies, they shall fail; whether there be tongues, they shall cease; whether there be knowledge, it shall vanish away". The distance was hard, the waiting game was strong. But we had love to get us through. Before long, all the wait was going to be over for good. No more doing all we can in one day because we only have six days. I was moving to the United States for good to be with my better half.

My husband may not be perfect, but his perfect imperfections are what makes him the person who he is. The person who calls on his lunch time to remind me how beautiful I am. The person who says, "babe, I am going to give you a minute to calm down" when I get upset, kiss me on the forehead and walks out of the room. He is same person who would give up his life for me without question. Yes, he may not fit in everyone's 'picture perfect husband's' frame but he is my person. The one I get to wake up with every single day for the rest of my life. He makes my journey worth it. I found him when I was looking for peace, finding myself and by doing such I found my everything in him. Once more, he is my person. For the rest of my life.

Chapter Nine

TRANSITIONING

People always use the phrase. "Change is hard". I mean, how hard can moving from middle school to high school be? Or moving from one apartment to the next? Or probably not so complex. How about changing your morning routine to fit in with being a new mom? Not so hard right? Well, let me tell you they are all hard. I have had experience with all except the latter, and as simple as they sound, they are very much challenging. You might question, why is doing something a little different comes under so much pressure? The answer is because getting out of one's comfort zone is hard. Comfort is a luxury my friend and people are not willing to give that up most of the time. But one thing we should always remember is that to grow our comfort must be disturbed or else we become stagnant. Growth is a necessity. Growth is vital. It will not be easy, but it surely will be worth it.

My family as I have mentioned in the earlier chapters is all I have known. We have our way of life. Eat the same food twice a week. Go to school, go to church, do my chores, respect my elders and peers etc. We live off the land and the natural resources around us for the most part and give back to such. My Jamaican culture and heritage were all I know and practice since the idea of ever living in a foreign country was more of a luxury for the rich and fortunate and I was not any of the above.

I had dreams of traveling to the United States sometime in the future if I was ever granted a visa, but never to reside. Canada was where I always fantasize about. I wanted to become a Registered Nurse and live there. That was the most that ever crossed my mind about a foreign land. Life sure does have a way of surprising us.

On December 15, 2018, I said my final goodbye to my parents and siblings. It was the most bittersweet day of my life. The fact that I would get to see my husband and not have to worry about how many days we got to spend together was great. But being away from my family for God knows how long was killing me. I keep telling myself it is okay, and we will video call all the time. But my strongest emotions were leading towards the kisses I would get at the airport after seeing my husband. I wanted to leave more than I wanted to stay at the time.

Even though my flight from the Sir Alexander Bustamante Airport in Montego Bay did not leave Jamaica until the 17th of December, I went to stay at my cousins in Ocho Rios for two nights in getting everything ready for the trip. I thought this was an amazingly effective decision since the taxi services in my hometown can be very scarce on a Sunday.

I experienced the longest two nights of my life. The 17th could not come fast enough. I was nauseous, I had diarrhea, I was just a mess. I have never been so nervous for nothing in my lifetime as I was to see my husband. After all I have not seen my husband after we went our separate way after our wedding. So, for the past six months there were a lot of built-up emotions. At one point I keep denying it. I told myself it was not happening; it was all a visit, and I would be back in Jamaica soon. I was not just packing all my stuff and leaving my family, my blood, my best friends and go. I could not bring myself to terms with it.

As the day slowly approaches, it gets more real. Here I was making homemade fry chicken and fish to bring to my husband. I was slicing up my mom's famous sweet potato pudding while my cousins boiled some ackee for me to take. It was all becoming real and there was nothing I could do to stop it. Or could I? Yes, I could! I could choose not to go see my husband. I could even ask for a breakup. None of which were viable options. But they were options none the least. At the time, which did not come to mind. I was missing my husband so bad, I was miserable. I would get triggered by the simplest of situations. I am not sure if it was hormones or what, but all I know I did not have them the day of the flight.

There I stand, in the line ready to check myself and my luggage in. Who move their entire life in two suitcases? Over 24 years of constantly being with family and doing the same thing every weekend was just all packed and ready to take on a new way of life. Was I ready though? Like ready to live in one of the country's coldest State, having bears, Moose and lynx surround me twenty-four seven? Oh, and please do not let me begin on them long summers days which lasted up to twenty-two hours of daylight and the long winter nights which falls from three thirty P.M in the afternoon. Simply put it was hard.

After hopping on my first flight from Jamaica to Atlanta, Georgia I was so elated. Yes, the waiting game to see my husband was over. I am ready. My flight was about three or four hours. I made it to Atlanta safely thank God. I then had a layover for another three hours before my connection flight leaves. I was so tired, and jet lagged but I could not bring myself to sleep. I was not going to miss my flight. As such I soldier on. Finally, it was boarding time.

As I sat in my seat, I started to reflect on the journey behind me and how far I came. The sacrifices I have made and my relentless efforts. For a second there I felt proud of the woman I was becoming. My flight from Georgia would take me another three to four hours to get to Denver, Colorado my second connection. That is now a total of eleven hours of just traveling. Denver international airport is the largest airport in the United States. It is always packed and busy. And what more busy time there is than in December when people are traveling back and forth to be with families for the Christmas season.

The four hours went by fast I must say, and I landed safely. It is always a blessing to see the aircraft come to a complete stop and everyone and everything is intact. As I escorted the aircraft, I thought to myself. How many people would make such a great sacrifice? And then it hits me. People do some of the craziest things known to man for love or even something that looks like love. And here I was upping my life and moving across the globe for love. Will it be worth it? Of course, it will. Well, at least in my case it was. One thing I was grateful for was the fact that I did not leave my family and friends on a bad term. I left in peace because I want to return with my new family some day in peace.

Denver was an experience. People everywhere. None stop movements of people missing their flight or too early for their flights. I was the latter. If you think sitting around waiting for three hours was bad, well, sorry to burst your bubble. My layover was 12 hours. I made it to the airport around 6pm on the 17th and my flight to Anchorage was not until 7Am on the 18th. The good thing was that I was tired, night was falling and whenever I wake up all I need to do was get on the plane. No paperwork, nothing.

I was exhausted and hungry. I keep updating my husband throughout the night, but he would soon fall asleep. At the time, Anchorage was two hours behind Denver. I thought I would just sleep through the twelve hours. I was wrong. I was not able to close my eyes for more than five minutes the most. How can I trust that no one is not going to try steal my personal stuff? Secondly, people are constantly walking past me. It was the most uncomfortable twelve hours of my life. I ordered food at the McDonald's restaurant, but I could not bring myself to have more than one bite of that soggy bread and stale chicken fried in refried oil. Then I remember I have fry chicken and fry fish in my purse. It was satisfying.

The hour has finally come for me to board my final flight. I dragged myself to my seat and struggle to put my overhead luggage away. I was losing strength. I finally got settled and was over the moon about it because now I feel more comfortable taking a nap. Well, I spoke on it too quickly. I napped for about an hour before got woken up by extreme turbulence. I got scared to the point of me sending goodbye text messages to my mom and my husband. Thankfully, they did not receive it until after I had already landed and call them.

I am not an enthusiastic fan of flying in an aircraft but because there is no other means of getting to my destinations, I always approached it with a smile. But when faced with turbulence that smile is nowhere in sight. I cried for a solid half an hour. It was the worst I have ever experienced. I thought that was going to be the end. But God has been strong for me once more. The turbulence was then over. I still could not get comfortable because I was saying to myself, "anytime now we could have another one" so it keeps me on my toes. Well, it was really the last one, but that was not where the troubles ended. Upon landing in Anchorage, the pilot announces that the clouds are hanging low so there was not much that he could see. Why would he have said that aloud with me already freaking out? My heart dropped once more. There was already more than a foot of snow in most places in Alaska. It was cloudy and ugly.

People starting to mutter and panicking hard while the flight attendants tried to calm everyone down. Bringing reassurance to us that everything will be all right. They tried, but over two hundred panicked voices were crying, drowning out the three flight assistants. I felt the wheels hit the runway. I looked through my window and could hardly see anything. It felt like a nightmare. The plane finally came to a complete stop, and everyone clapped, commend the pilots and starts smiling again. For a minute it wanted to watch a horror movie. I messaged my husband immediately to let him know that I made it safe. My internet was down so once more he did not receive it.

As I make my way off the aircraft, my anxiety kicks in. I was going out of breath, getting tears in my eyes and extremely nervous. All I had was to do now was go to the baggage claim area, pick up my luggage and wait for my husband. But before that, I had to rush to the powder room. Did my final makeup touch ups, brush my teeth, apply perfume and wash my hands? I was shaking like a leaf. As I make my way down the escalator, I saw the cutest face with the most gorgeous smile looking at me. How did he get there so fast? Frank, I did not care. I was glad he was there waiting for me. I ran down the escalator because it was too slow for me. I dropped my phone, my purse and everything I was carrying and crashed in his arms. His arms wrapped around my body like a newborn in a blanket. I cried, he cried it was just a priceless moment.

So, remember when I asked myself earlier if I was ready for this transition? Turns out I was not. After collecting my luggage, we made our way to his truck. He was parked in the overhead garage right outside the exit. He was now six feet away from me because when I first set foot outside the cold was unbearable, so I backed up. He realized I was no longer behind him and offer to pull his truck down to the doorway. I was not ready for a below freezing type of climate. That day it was nineteen degrees in Anchorage and the day I left Jamaica it was 91 degrees. Dramatic difference. I wore a flip flop, a very thin leggings and a plaid long sleeve. All of which are not recommended for Alaska's weather. I did not bring even one relatively warm piece of clothing with me. After all, everything I owned was in the category skirt or dress because of religious reasons at the time. I sneak the leggings in my suitcase from a year before.

We quickly got settled, got our own apartment and started adjusting. Merging both our lives into one with a lot of compromises. At first it felt amazing. New home, meeting new people etc. But as the months go by, I started to miss home. My parent's birthdays would come along, family dinners, family reunion, Mother's Day, Father's Day among others and everyone except me was there. That was the hardest thing I struggled with and is still struggling with while adjusting to a new way of life. I am the one who baked all the birthday cakes, helped with family dinners and events and here I was not able to do any of the above.

I would wake up at nights crying about it. I would make dinner and not eat. I crave their presence so bad I would just call them just to hear their voices. Not only was I stressing myself, but it was affecting my husband as well. It bothers him to see me like that and make him feel as though I do not want to be there with him. And even though he understands the closeness of the relationship between my family and I, he knew the path I was going down was not a healthy one. And as such, he tried to find things to do that I would enjoy with him and distract my mind for a while. We would go bowling, night dates, coffee dates etc. It surely helped. Overtime I understand that it is okay to miss them but to crave their attention constantly was going to form a much bigger problem as they have their daily lives and families to tend to as well.

Chapter Ten

HEAD ABOVE THE WATERS

I have grown up swimming in the Thomas River for all my childhood and young adult life. It is extremely easy for me to swim and maneuver myself out of any drowning situation or to help someone in that situation. I have had rough days in that river. From chasing clothing that get away while washing, fetching breadfruits or sudden River swelling, I have seen it all. When you are not in any of those situations you have a whole escape route for the "what if's". But, surrounded by that chaos, eventually forces you to think and act fast. For all that I have experienced there is one key rule, no matter what you do keep your head above the water. Very sadly, not many people know how to do this. When we are faced with challenging times, our instinct is to shut down, feel alone, think no one cares or there cannot be a feasible way out. We questioned where we went wrong in our lives, what have we done to deserve some very unfortunate situations that have been presented to us and so on. When you are like me who have been dished my fair Share of struggles, you have no choice other than to make it out of every drowning situation alive. Look at it like the universe has somewhat against you, and every day you wake up it is a brand-new day to prepare yourselves for the struggles ahead. A positive mindset is an immensely powerful thing.

One would have thought, at this point in the book, after all the childhood struggles, lost friendship, untrusted family's things are starting to look up. Well, not so much. The hardest days are only ahead of me. My university journey as I mentioned earlier is still to date one of my hardest struggles. In November of 2017 I was scheduled to graduate from the University of The West Indies, Mona, Jamaica. After participating on the J1 work and travel program in the United State in May of that said year, I was notified through my school portal that I had failed a course that would require me to utilize two full semesters. Bear in mind that I have prepared for graduation and feeling accomplished to complete university on my scheduled time. Only to find out that I must spend another year for one course.

At that point in time, I felt as if I was going to die. The constant chest pain, headaches, diarrhea, I have experienced it all. And even though I was in the United States working and making new friends, meeting my current husband and going on adventures, a part of me was still empty and hurting. I could not get over the fact that I won't be able to graduate on time. I really felt as though I should have just given up but when I look at all the sacrifices my families have made just to send me through university, all the late nights I have been up studying and getting work done, I had no choice than to pick up where I left off and carry on. I was so determined to succeed I had was to take a break from close friends and family. I was hungry for it. And as such I distant myself from every possible distraction. My first day walking into that lecture room, September 2017 I was angry, I was hurting, I was bitter. I should not be in that room; I should be sending out job applications and fixing to graduate the November. For that entire year I spend three hours two days a week for that one course. I saw it as pointless and frustrating, but I still push. The next may came around and it was examination time. I was confident but was also a bit worried. This specific course is known to have university students spending years trying to pass it.

The day came and I finally sat in front of my paper. I remember praying to God asking him for his leading and direction in completing this exam and grant unto me the victory. After the exam was over, I now must focus on getting everything ready for my second J1 work and travel program in the United States. I was excited for a lot of reasons. For one, it was my sister's first time traveling on an airplane and visiting the United States. Secondly, I was only a month out from my wedding, and thirdly I was going to see my best friend of fourteen years that I have not seen in a while, so yes. I was very stoked. But somewhere in the middle of all that, I was a nervous wreck. Results was published in June, right before my wedding. I remember my only college friend Kim, texting me that the results are out, and I should check. My chest tightens up, I am running out of breath. Everything was going right, and I could not afford to fail again. I enter my username and password into my school's portal. I scroll as slow as I could until I reach the bottom. I looked and there it was, a big fat B+. I was never one of those students who beat themselves up because they missed the A+ by two Marks.

I was always grateful for every C that I have ever received knowing that I passed a course, and I am moving forward. I could not contain myself. I stand up in my bed and was just screaming. My sister was not home at the time, but I could not help but feel like the house was filled with my relatives all cheering me on. I felt relieved. My heart was full, and finally I can walk down the aisle with a light heart to meet my husband. I had the best days at work the days after finding out the results. I was not so tense anymore; I smile a lot more and was just more pleasant. As time goes by, I forgot about it. I had my wedding, I get to see my best friend, life was good. Well, not so fast. As the time comes for my sister and I to go back to

Jamaica, I could not help but wonder, where is my congratulations email from my university telling me about graduation and all the minute details. It was now September, and I am becoming uneasy. I called the school trying to find out what was going on. I was told that notification can sometimes takes longer to reach out to some persons so I should just wait and see. Okay, I guess I will just have to wait then. After all they have thousands of students to attend to, so my notification email will be in sometime soon.

Once again, I quickly forget about it since I was on my way to Florida from Missouri to spend some time with my best friend who flew all the way to Missouri for my wedding. I was mostly focused on spending time and just catching up with her and her family. I would occupy my days when she left for work with just about anything I could do around the house, go to church with the family on Saturdays and on her days off we would go somewhere fun or grab a bite. So, yes, I was not so concerned about not getting my confirmation email from my school. Time went by fast, and it was now the ending of September and I have only two days before I leave for Jamaica on the first of October 2018. I started to get worried again. By this time, I have seen a lot of my colleagues posting their confirmation email all over social media so now I am worried. Finally, I made it back to Jamaica and ready to figure out what was going on, so I went straight to my dean's office to get some clarity. Walking in that room I had so much confidence. For one I have the required credits to make the graduation list, so I was not worried. I had all my main courses and electives so again nothing to be troubled about. It is probably some misunderstanding in their system, it happens all the time. I remember my Dean of Discipline asked me for my full name and ID number.

It suddenly became noticeably quiet with just the sound of the computer's keyboard. For about ten minutes he could not see what the problem was because everything looks good, or that was what we thought. We finally discovered what was the issue, but there was no uncomplicated way of telling me that I was short a second- or third-year elective. They required twenty second- or third-year courses and I have nineteen. And instead of having ten first year courses I have eleven. How could that be though. Then it came to me. When choosing an elective, I did not know it has to be a level two or three course. So, when I chose a level one, it did not contribute to my degree at all. I literally wet myself right there in the Dean's office. I could not believe what I was hearing, I rushed to the bathroom crying my eyes out. When I composed myself and walk back to the Dean's office all I felt was pain and shame. Pain of all sorts, I could have died. My first instinct was to get out of that office, out of that school and never go back. But instead, I asked what I need to do to fix this problem.

Remember it was now October and school has been going on for over a month now. The first option was to just register for a second or thirst year course, anyone. And get it over with or wait until the January to do it. I was so ready with being out of that school I went for the first option. I tried registering for so many courses with no luck. They were all full since classes were going on for about 6 weeks now. I gave up for that semester. It was now December of 2018, and my husband was in the middle of doing my paperwork for me to migrate to the United States. I went back over to my university and explained my situation and asked if it was possible for me to sit an exam from overseas. I got a lot of useful information and the go ahead. I came to the US to reside permanently on December eighteen of 2018. It was a new thing for me, happy to see my husband whom I have not seen for the past six months so I was excited. None the less I was extremely focused on finding a course that would allow me to get the notes online and sit the exam here in the United States. Thank Goodness, I finally found one. It was remarkably like a lot of the previous courses I did so that was a good start for me.

I did all my course work, got my grades and everything was going well. Now it was time for my final exam. I have gone ahead and set up a proctor and a location for the exam while confirming it with the examination sections at the University of the West Indies. I have also paid my fee to get the exam paper shipped to me here in Alaska. The big day has arrived. All I need to focus on is passing this elective and I will have my degree awarded in the following May. I checked in Thirty minutes before my exam time just to make sure everything was going smoothly. Only to find out my paper did not make it to the location. I paid for expedited shipping and even then, it was not there. I was so upset. It was like every time I make one step closer in finishing university, I fall fifty steps back. The proctor console me and told me she will do her best to find a way for me to sit the exam. After about an hour passed my schedule time, she finally gets in touch with someone from my university about it. We were so happy thinking this is it now. To our surprise she would not provide the code needed for the soft copy version because Alaska was Four hours behind Jamaica's time zone and the exam was already started in Jamaica. I have so much anger built up I could just burst in two.

After I pay to have the examination paper reaching the location on time and it didn't, and hours of trying to get in touch with someone from my school and nothing, I now must pay the consequences of something I did not contribute to. I called my mom in tears and pain. I did not know what else to do. How many times must I allow myself to be pushed over and trampled on. I told my husband that was it and I was done with this University thing. He was there to encourage me to go on. My mom was able to console me. I could not help but feel that I was being punished by God for turning my back on him. I could hear my pastor's voice saying, "when God needs you and you turn your back on him, he will let you can't pass a single subject in school". I could not get it out of my head for a long while.

September of 2019 came, and I decided to try it again. Just like the previous times I did my course work, received my grades things were going fine. It was now December, and results will be out any day now. Unlike the previous time, I was excited I kept checking. I was more confident in passing this course. I logged into my account and scroll all the way to the bottom. My mouth was opened wide. I did not know what to do in that moment with what I saw. It was not that I failed a course, it was that my final exam was not graded. My head began to hurt now. What could possibly cause this? Could it be that the proctor here did not fax my paper over to the university? Why am I so unlucky? I started asking myself these questions. I could not bring myself to cry because again, things like these happen, I just need to call and figure out what was going on. As such I started communicating with the same lady who has helped me to get everything sorted out at my university. She was able to find my paper and my grades. My paper was marked, and the grades was imputed, but they were not sent to my faculty.

Hearing that has taken a gigantic load off my head but still has not put me at ease because I was not sure if I passed, or I have failed. She was not able to tell me what my grade was, but she told me not to worry I did not need to re-sit it. That was all I needed to know so I took comfort in that. She assured me that she will take care of it, and I will be able to see my exact grade within the next twenty-four hours. They said third time is the charm and it was true. Everything went smoothly while staying on top of my game double checking I was going to be finished this time for good. Twenty-four hours went by and there it was, my Bachelor of Sciences degree, majoring in Public Policy and Management was awarded. I cried and cried and then cried some more.

My husband took me out to this elite restaurant and treat me like a queen. For all my arduous work and resilience was paid off. That chapter of my life has ended with a lot of lessons learnt that I am now able to impart to individuals in similar situations. And even though I managed to keep my head up above the waters and ride out my storm, it non the less came with a lot of pain and sacrifice. It took a lot of sacrifice and patience to get through.

As if trying to keep my head above the water to get my degree was not bad enough for me, how about having me struggle with my United States residency, send my husband ten thousand miles away from me for a month in the peak of winter and then top it all off with a global pandemic. Just awesome right! Not. I would not say that I have become accustomed to fighting for everything in my life, because I have not. I would say though I have become more aware that at any time during the process things can turn south for me. In all my experiences that is how it has always been.

After making it to Alaska in December of 2018, it was no bed of roses. Physically, emotionally and financially. The snow was knee high in a lot of places and nineteen degrees Celsius below freezing. It was horrible. I had a twenty-seven-hour flight over the course of two days and was just about ready to get some rest and quality time with my husband, only to find out the hotel he had in mind for us while we search for apartments was now booked out. We were then referred to an apartment style hotel with kitchen and laundry room for Two hundred dollars per week. I personally think that was too expensive but, in that moment, we really did not have a chance. You might be wondering where my husband was staying at the time. Let me bring you up to speed. My husband Billy Barthol III was serving in the Army and stationed at the Joint-Base Elmendorf Richardson base here in Alaska.

As a result, he was living on the military base in the barracks. Visitors are forbidden from staying there. Well, if they find out. My first three days I was emotionally exhausted after waking up at nine AM only to find outside pitch black. That was new to me. It was now the Saturday and my husband decided that we were going to his barracks room to grab some detergent for laundry. Upon arriving there, we realized that it would be nicer if I stayed there. He had his own bathroom and kitchen area, closer to his work and I did not have any reason to be outside. We then went back to the hotel for my belongings. It was exciting but scary, nonetheless. If I were seen in his room, it would have resulted in a huge chaos. So, all I did was make dinner, take care of the house and binge watch 'Switch at Birth' the entire time.

This specific day as I am enjoying the second episode, I saw my phone lit up with messages from my husband. A lot of messages. It was not pleasant to read. There was an ongoing room inspection that day that he had just found out about. There is hardly any place to hide than to shut myself in the bathroom. Thank goodness he got one of his friends to remove his inspection chart from his door, resulting in the room not being checked and classified as vacant. That was a narrow escape. It makes me very uneasy and uncomfortable.

At first, we liked the idea of not paying rent for a chance to save more, but the risks were too great. We spent about a month and a half in the barracks then we found a one-bedroom apartment and moved out. Having our own place brings more peace to our soul. Our first night was not the most comfortable because we did not have nothing more than a TV and memory foam mattress, but it was filled with love, and affection that we were able to share with each other. As the months goes by, we start filling up our space with furniture until we were both contented. Life was good and it was now time to move on to the next stage, getting my Permanent residency in the United States.

The process of filing for a permanent residency status can be a hectic one. Not to mention the cost. This is not something you can just sit around and decide to get it done whenever you feel to. It is in a time scale. When you enter the US, you have one hundred and eighty days, approximately six months to submit all fees and paperwork before asked to depart the country. At the time coming up with one thousand three hundred was hard to come by when that is more than half of my husband's paycheck. Time was against us, and it was now may, and I only have until June 16th, 2019.

I was desperate but I know even then I would not ask for help from either side of the family. I get to work and start researching. It was then that I found a lady who work on the Military base who assist families in this process. That was some good news for us. We head out the following day and found her office. Well, it was not what we expected. She helped families in filling out the forms, answer immigration related questions and so on. I am not saying we did not need that kind of help, but those were things we could take care of ourselves. We need financial assistance.

After my husband discovered that she was not able to help us, he became frustrated and wanted us to leave. Leaving did not feel like the right thing to do. I dropped my pride and began to open to her about our situation. Who would have taught that she would have known someone just one door away that could have helped us? Mr. Michael Baty. This veteran is one of the founders of the Army Emergency Relief. (AER loan). He welcomed us with an open arm and listened as we plead our case. After about thirty minutes, it was time to check if we have qualified for a loan. It was hard to pinpoint for a few minutes because of some misunderstanding about our needs. He would now have to file our report to the Sargent major to see if it were lined up with their standard.

Now the waiting game begins. The two days waiting for an answer were the longest days of my life. I could not stay put. My husband finally gets the messaged and it was approved. A weight has just lifted off our shoulders. And even though it was another waiting game, we were not worried since we had already explained the deadline we were working with. Thankfully, we have received the check two weeks before the deadline. I have already gone ahead and filled out all the forms we would need, or that was what we thought. For some reason it was taking a while for us to cash the check since our bank is in another state. What we did not know was that could have easily scanned the barcode and have it deposited directly to our account.

It was now June 14th on a Friday, and I am already angry at my husband for trying to do everything last minute. We made it to the post office and ready to send in our documents. We were informed that it is guaranteed two days delivery and we were happy that it was going to be delivered on the 16th. About three months went by and we heard nothing, now we are starting to get worried. In the fourth month we got a letter stating they received and approved our application. Breakthrough for us.

Now we could just relax and trust the timing that everything was going to work out. Another two months we heard nothing. On January 2 we received a letter in the mail. We were a nervous wreck. What could this be now. It was within that six-month period where you would normally be given the final notice and an interview date. I remember my husband and I sat in the truck nervously opening the letter. It became noticeably silent. Not a single word then I saw my husband threw everything away and becomes emotional. He was angry. That was all I need to know that something was not right.

He then said that they have denied my case and I got thirty days to file an appeal or a motion to reopen the case. To do any of the above, I first need to know why my case was denied. I have been a lawful resident, no crime nothing. After reading the letter, we were informed that our case was denied because of failure to submit an affidavit of support form. What? That

137

cannot be true because we have copies of everything we sent in, so it must be a mistake.

We start researching about that form and found out the sad truth. Yes, we did not provide an affidavit of support form, instead we provided three samples of affidavits letters from friends and families. How was this our fault though, we were guided and instructed by the individual helping us in the military base. Right here and then, our world crumbled. We are already struggling financially, how are we going to come up with that kind of money again within thirty days? It was impossible. After my husband done his research, we realized we do not have to start all over again and it would not be as expensive.

As such we file an I-290B motion to reopen our case. We were able to get a grant this time from the AER loans which we did not have to repay. Going this route can sometimes can be very scary and persons usually get an immigration lawyer to plead their case. We could not afford a lawyer, so I start putting pen to paper. After I was finished, I would then have five pages of unadulterated truth as to why that form was not submitted and begged for a second chance.

Dealing with this chaos is usually hard but when you have your partner there to embrace you through it, it always hurts a little less. Well, that was all about to change in a matter of days. My husband was scheduled for a thirty-day training event starting on January 3rd, just a day after we received the denial notice. How can he leave in a time like this? He was panicking and crying. For some reason I could not bring myself to cry, I had was to be strong for him. He was so worried about losing me, thinking they were going to send me back to Jamaica. He started reaching out to his Sargent explaining the situation. He was granted some extra days to deal with family matters. I appreciate his superiors a lot for that opportunity. We managed to take care of it and send it the required documents and fees on the twenty-two of January 2020. It was now a waiting game once more.

Now that my husband was away, I had time to really process everything. I cried some days and smiled the others. It was now approaching the peak of winter and here I was home alone, without a Job, not being able to drive my husband truck because I did not have a license at the time. I felt helpless. I met a couple friends here that we hang out with once every three month that would come pick me up and take me grocery shopping or just hang out. I was very thankful for their courtesy. Not only is it freezing cold but it's also very dark. We were only getting three to four hours max of daylight time, so just imagine waking up in the dark and by you can finish making lunch it is once again dark. It gets lonely and depressing extremely fast. In those time I spend my days reading and staying in touch with my families. My husband was extremely far away from me, but he would make it a duty to talk to me every night before bed. It soothes a lot of my emotional pain. It brings comfort.

In February, my husband made it back home. It was genuinely nice to have some normalcy again. He was given a couple of days to just relax and unwind from that training event and oh how we enjoyed that time. Not long after my husband made it back home, we received another letter from the Immigration services. Ever since that denial letter, we became scared of opening any letter concerning the immigrations. To our surprise it was some good news. While they have denied my permanent residency, we had filed together my workers authorization separately. So that letter was just informing us that my worker's authorization card will be coming in the mail soon. This was not my green card, but I was excited to have given the opportunity to work while I wait in my Permanent Residency.

Wait! Not so fast. Here comes a global pandemic. What does the universe need from me? It has always been one thing

139

after the next. I was so relieved that we could make both ends meet easily with me getting a job but what are the odds that I would have received your permit to work, just in the time when businesses are shutting down and laying off their current employees. Why was I so surprised though? 2020 has been one of my most trying years, with one thing after the other. So here I was with my permit to work but could not get a job. After a while I start looking at the greater good. What if some higher powers were just protecting me from getting a job that would put me at risk to the Corona virus? I still to this day have no idea but cannot help but be grateful. For health, for family, for life. I could have gone out there and die. But even with a couple of thousands of dollars less, having life and spending time with the ones you love is still of a greater value. It was not easy to think like that in the beginning when all I see is bills that needs to get paid.

As the pandemic spike up in April of 2020 here in Alaska and around the world, individuals were required to stay home and self-quarantine. No traveling, no outdoors gathering or anything like that. Within this time, everything feels down. We must now start adjusting to a new normal of wearing a face mask when going out in the public along with gloves, maintaining six feet apart, washing our hands for at least twenty seconds among the list of many other protocols in maintaining the spread of such a deadly virus. How does someone keep their head above the waters when they are laid off, cannot afford to pay their rent, got evicted in the peak of winter and cannot feed their families? It has been hard on a lot of us. I was grateful for the fact that my husband's job still allows him to work from home for the most part while still getting his full pay to care of our home and family.

In a matter of days, what we then knew as normal was taken away from us just like that. We quickly adjusted to the new normalcy. We did not really have the choice. The level of panic surrounding the virus started to weigh on me. I would have anxiety reading about it. It became just too much for me. As I result, I stopped reading articles related to it and stop checking the count in my state. It was hard to do at first, but I managed to succeed and never looked back. I start becoming more appreciative of every day that I get to wake up with my soulmate.

Within this time both my husband and I were starting to get a little worried about my permanent residency situation. With everything shutting down we were positive that we would not be hearing from immigration in a while. It was now August and the last letter we received was in June confirming that they had received some extra evidence that we had sent in. I went on the internet to see if I could find even a tiny ray of hope as to what may be happening, and there it was. The United States Citizens and Immigration services (USCIS) were ceasing all work due to a furlough they wanted sign and passed by the Congress. In other words, they were going on a strike from all work until a sum of money is being paid to them. I was so down but at the same type it gave me some hope that I was not alone in the waiting game.

About a week passed and I was going about my normal days, buying stuff off Amazon and keeping up with the social life. I had some packages coming in the mail, so I went to pick them up. I was surprised to see an immigration letter. How is this possible? I was not supposed to be receiving a letter since the immigration services are down. Anyways, I quickly rushed back to the car and quickly forget about everything I bought and start ripping apart the envelope. What could possibly go wrong now? I thought to myself. As I start reading my heart starts pounding fast, I wanted to pee so bad. The very first two sentences changed my life. That day I received an interview date for September 1st,2020; and would then receive my green card two weeks after. I remember rushing into the house to share my good news with my husband. We hugged and cried then laugh. It has been a very rough year for us from the start

141

and this was a major relief. We could not keep our good news to ourselves, so I started calling my family and my husband did the same. We were excited.

The letter state that I should have a medical exam done and bring the results with me on the day of the appointment. That was an easy thing for us, or that was what we thought. This examination is a very in depth one and was going to require my immunization card which was in Jamaica at the time. I quickly called my mom and then I remember, for a while I had it in some of my college belongings after moving back in my mom's house and then it got lost. So here we were on a time watch missing a very crucial piece of information card.

My mom being the most resilient and trying person did not just sit and wallow in the moment. She gets working for me. She visited the clinic where I was registered but it was not there due to reconstruction on the building, it was at a different location in storage. She then visited my high school and thankfully she was able to get a copy printed that she could have brought to the clinic and have them ruled up a brand-new card for me. My sisters then send me the card through expedited shipping which make it to me within two days. When I finally get ahold of it in my hands, I was so stoked. Now I do not have to worry no more.

Well, not so fast. I managed to set an appointment about a week and a half before my appointment date. When the date came and I showed up, it was a big running around. Doctors not sure if the services the immigration requested were offered at that hospital and so on. After an hour there I got word that they will be able to do. Finally. I was instructed to go to the immunization section to have my information imputes in the form, easy one two three. Well, once again not so easy. Upon reaching there the nurse asked me if the records in my immunization card all were, I have and I told her yes. She then told me the USCIS needs more so I will have to get some shots and some rest done. Okay I can work with that. I quickly asked about the steps of moving forward and was helped by her in getting the shot that I needed. I now must do two different blood tests. I was just ready to get everything done so I made it to the lab.

As I made it to the window and explained my reasons for being there, I was told they were out of one of the tests. Holy hell! Not right now when I do not have that kind of time. I was sad but I just went on and did the one that were available. After completing that test, I was informed that I would then get the results within two to three weeks. My eyes were opened wide. I only have a week before my interview, and I would need all these results to bring in with me.

For a second, I started to panic then I composed myself and thought. This is not your first set back; you have always found a way out. You are strong, you are a fighter, you will win. I came home and reread the letter once more just searching for anything that could help. And there it works in bold. The letter state that for any reason a person cannot make it to the interview they should call a specific number to reschedule an appointment or if one is experiencing any symptoms of COVID 19.

It has just been two days since my husband was placed on restriction of movement because he had come in contact someone who was exposed to a positive case. I quickly get on the phone, explained my case and reschedule my appointment. A week after I received a letter with a new appointment date for September 21,2020. I was overjoyed. Now we have enough time to get the results back and the medical examination completed. I finally received the call from my nurse to pick up my documents. What a relief.

September 21st eight fifteen AM my husband and I stand in line outside the Unites States Citizens and Immigration Services office (USCIS). We were inspected as a requirement for safety and following the CDC guidelines in controlling the spread of the Corona Virus. As we went in and nervously sat six feet away from my each other, I could not help but wonder how hard this interview was going to be. Will they terrorize me? Will my husband panic and say the wrong answer? I was a ball of nerves. It was now time for me to go inside. My husband was asked to stay out. My interview lasted for about thirty minutes mainly double checking all my documents were adding up. I was asked three questions total. What was my mother-in-law birthday, her given name and address?

Normally when someone filed for their permanent residency status (green card) and it is approved, they get a total of two years then they will have to do the full process again and then qualify for ten years if they have kept a clean record. So, I was prepared for the two years. I was grateful that I can now travel back to my home country Jamaica whenever I want. As my interview was ending, my interviewer said to me that I should expect the card in my mailbox within the next thirty days. I said OK and start packing up my stuff.

She then said, "wait, you just got lucky. You will not be getting the two years card since you are married for over two years on the date of the interview you will be getting the ten years one". Did I just fell asleep in this lady's office and is in dream and illusion? On June 30th, 2020, my husband and I celebrated two years of marriage and three years of togetherness. So earlier on that January when our case was denied, it pushed us over the two years mark qualifying us for a full ten years of legal residency. I cried so hard.

I rushed out to the car that my husband was waiting in with the biggest smile on my face. That was enough proof to tell him it went well but he did not know I have some bigger news for him. We hugged and he asked how it went. I told him it went better than I expected and them told him the good news. He could not believe what I was saying. We cried in each other's arm and then celebrated with some nice wine and whiskey. The phone calls began once more. We called our families together to share the good news. It was a lot of emotions. This rollercoaster was over. For good this time. How did that situation and all other contributing factors did not drown us? God has been strong for us. It was at that moment we looked backed and all the mishaps, all the roadblocks and denials were working in our favor for a greater good.

When I talk about how God has been there for me throughout my whole life, I do not say it because it is easy to say, or I heard someone else said it. I had personal experience with a lot of drowning situations. Situations that I should not have made it out of or made it out alive. Because there is a difference. Not everyone makes it out alive in drowning situations. For some it permanently perplexes their mindset, they cannot see pass the pain, they became stagnant as a person. Not been able to facilitate growth and as a result is able to transpire that energy to everyone that comes around them. For me, they make me stronger, they opened my eyes to the mentality of anything can happen any minute now. I became more resilient, more willing to fight back and more courageous.

What can I say? It has been a very rough year, better yet rough life. But the more struggles present themselves to me the more I fight. I cannot give up. Not now, not ever. What is your strongest suit in self growth? What makes you look at yourself and think, this is what builds me, this is what makes me who I am. For me personally, my strongest suit is the will to fight back. I cannot see myself settling. It is one of my greatest motivations. Drowning situations always brings about some form of panic.

So, this is what I have always tell myself. If I cannot currently see a way how to get out of my drowning situation, I will not cry for help putting someone else's life at risk. I said this to say, in the physical concept of drowning, if you do not have the right skills in saving a drowning person, that same person can cause both persons to drown. As a result, I do not

145

throw my problems on my husband or family while panicking because they will not know how to help me.

I must suppress all that worry and convince them that everything will be all right while dying inside. It is the same as just floating on the water. It makes it easier for the person coming to rescue you when you are not splashing all over the place in panic. When I am calm and collective, I have now opened myself for suggestions and guidance on how to get out of a drowning situation. I then weighed all my options then divert to the best one.

Telling you not to panic in your drowning situations would be too unfair of me, as someone who has done their fair share of panicking. Being human beings that is our instinct and will always be our first resort. But what I can say is that one should try to panic as little as possible. In this case, it makes it easier to get out. Think of it like quicksand. The more you panicked about going under the faster you sank. Try to compose yourself. You will come out with some bruises, even some broken bones sometimes. You may even feel the need to cry, to crawl or to run, but whatever you do, keep your head above the waters.

Made in the USA
Columbia, SC
06 September 2022

66087257R00080